MELCHESTER ROVERS

REBELLION

Creative Director and CEO: Jason Kingsley
Chief Technical Officer: Chris Kingsley
Head of Books & Comics: Ben Smith
Roy of the Rovers Brand Manager: Rob Power
Roy of the Rovers Editor: Keith Richardson
Graphic Design: Sam Gretton

Published by Rebellion,
Riverside House, Osney Mead, Oxford, OX2 0ES, UK.
www.rebellionpublishing.co.uk

Manufactured in Ukraine by Imago.

First Printing: March 2019
10 9 8 7 6 5 4 3 2 1

www.royoftheroversofficial.com
royoftheroversofficial royoftheroversofficial royoftherovers

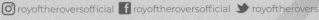

ROY OF THE ROVERS®

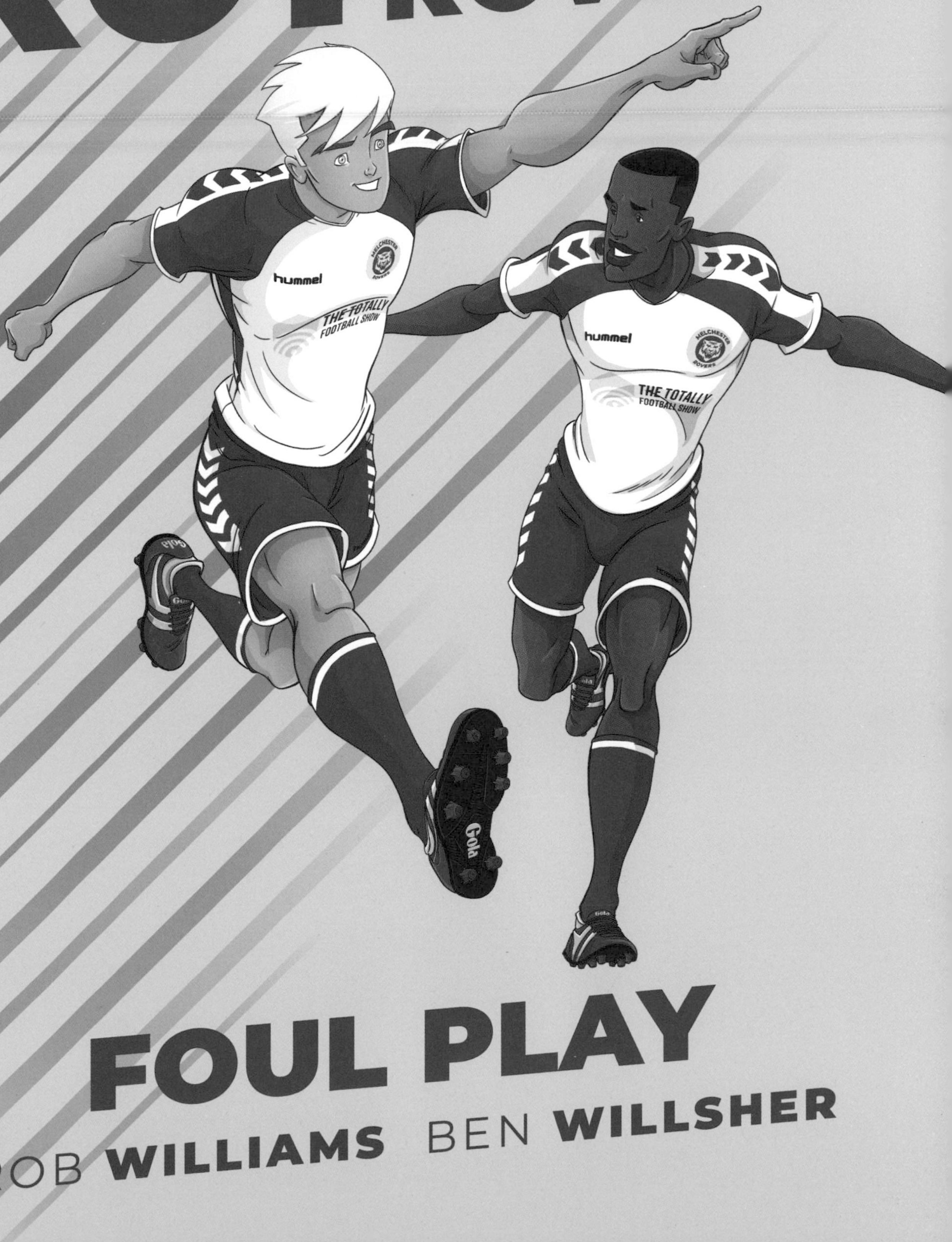
hummel
THE TOTALLY FOOTBALL SHOW
hummel
THE TOTALLY FOOTBALL SHOW
MELCHESTER ROVERS
Gola

FOUL PLAY

ROB **WILLIAMS** BEN **WILLSHER**

BOOK TWO
FOUL PLAY

Script
ROB WILLIAMS

Art
BEN WILLSHER

Letters
JIM CAMPBELL

Colours
JOHN CHARLES & **GUILHERME LINDEMBERG MENDES**

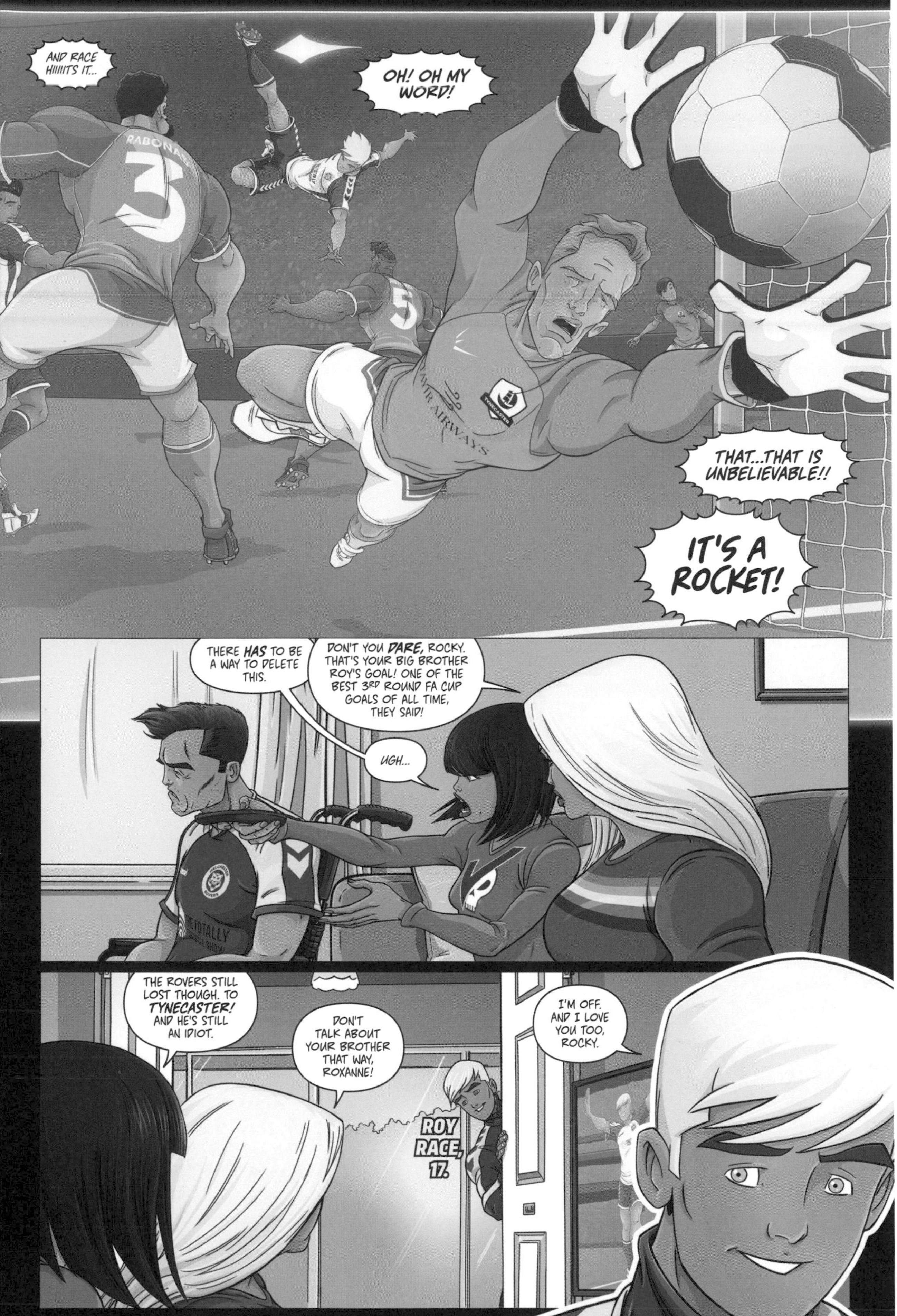
AND RACE HIIIIITS IT...
OH! OH MY WORD!
RABONAS
THAT...THAT IS UNBELIEVABLE!!
IT'S A ROCKET!
THERE HAS TO BE A WAY TO DELETE THIS.
DON'T YOU DARE, ROCKY. THAT'S YOUR BIG BROTHER ROY'S GOAL! ONE OF THE BEST 3RD ROUND FA CUP GOALS OF ALL TIME, THEY SAID!
UGH...
THE ROVERS STILL LOST THOUGH. TO TYNECASTER! AND HE'S STILL AN IDIOT.
DON'T TALK ABOUT YOUR BROTHER THAT WAY, ROXANNE!
I'M OFF. AND I LOVE YOU TOO, ROCKY.
ROY RACE, 17.

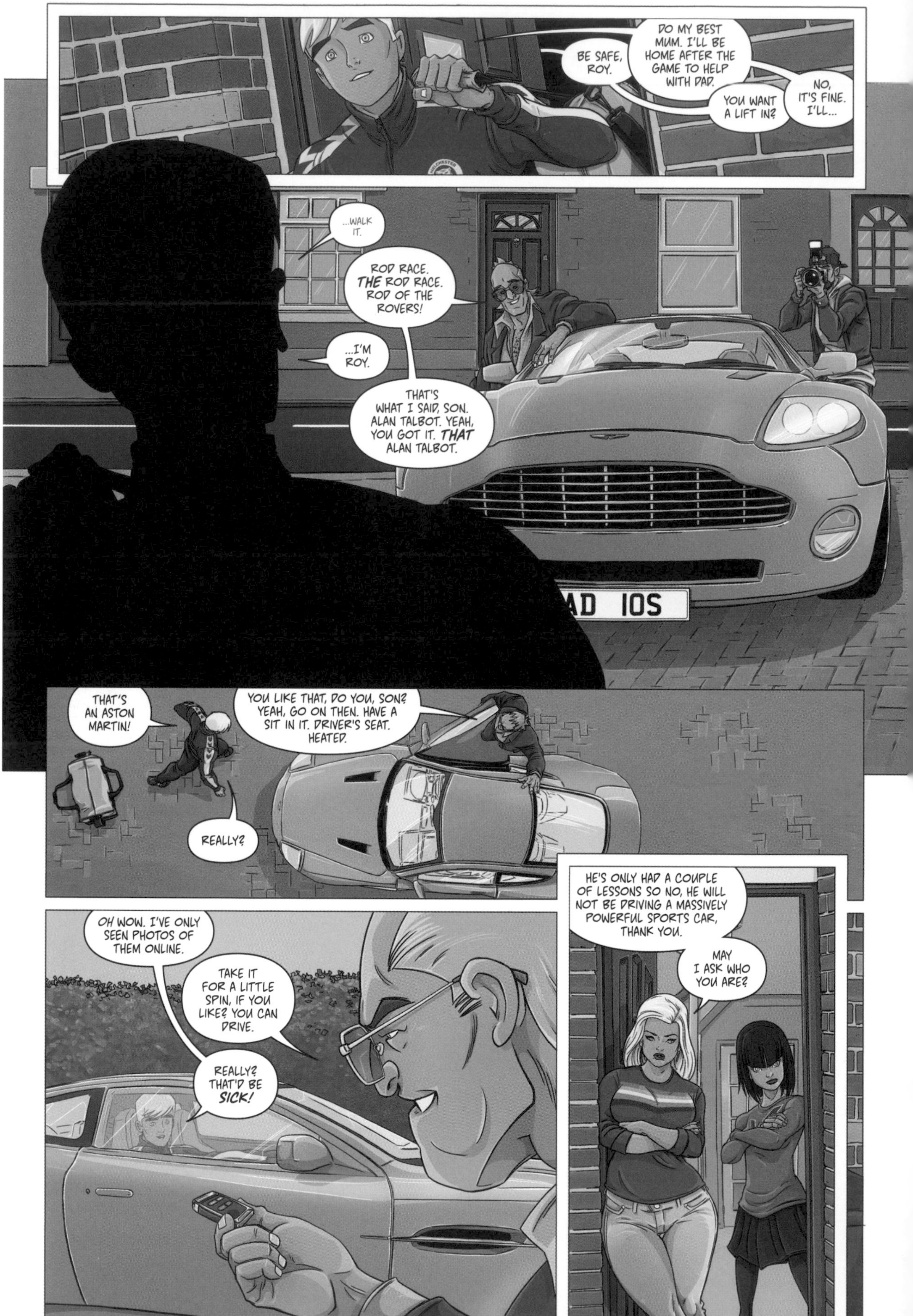
BE SAFE, ROY.
DO MY BEST MUM. I'LL BE HOME AFTER THE GAME TO HELP WITH DAD.
YOU WANT A LIFT IN?
NO, IT'S FINE. I'LL...
...WALK IT.
ROD RACE. THE ROD RACE. ROD OF THE ROVERS!
...I'M ROY.
THAT'S WHAT I SAID, SON. ALAN TALBOT. YEAH, YOU GOT IT. THAT ALAN TALBOT.
AD IOS
THAT'S AN ASTON MARTIN!
YOU LIKE THAT, DO YOU, SON? YEAH, GO ON THEN. HAVE A SIT IN IT. DRIVER'S SEAT. HEATED.
REALLY?
OH WOW. I'VE ONLY SEEN PHOTOS OF THEM ONLINE.
TAKE IT FOR A LITTLE SPIN, IF YOU LIKE? YOU CAN DRIVE.
REALLY? THAT'D BE SICK!
HE'S ONLY HAD A COUPLE OF LESSONS SO NO, HE WILL NOT BE DRIVING A MASSIVELY POWERFUL SPORTS CAR, THANK YOU.
MAY I ASK WHO YOU ARE?

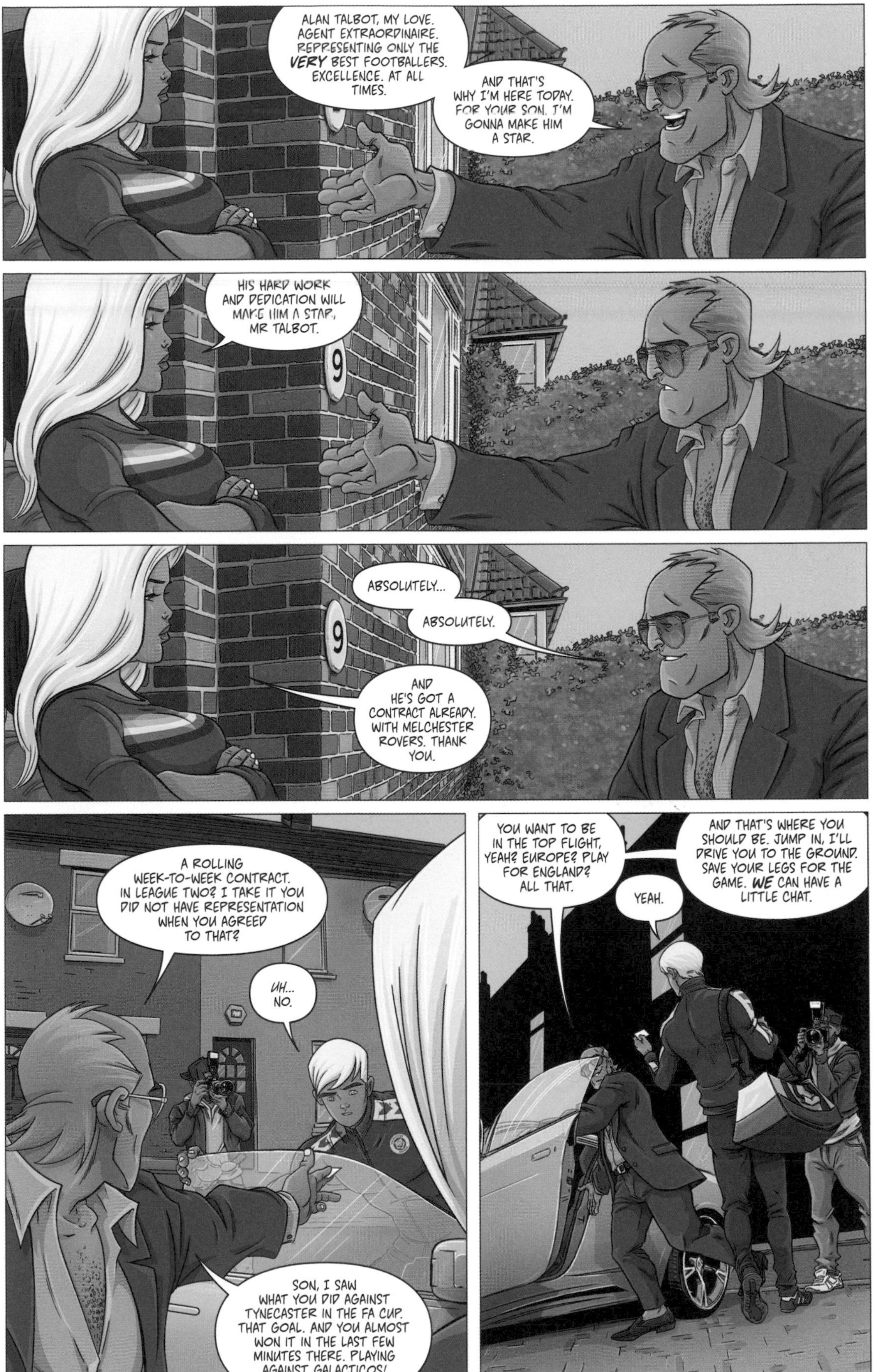
ALAN TALBOT, MY LOVE. AGENT EXTRAORDINAIRE. REPRESENTING ONLY THE VERY BEST FOOTBALLERS. EXCELLENCE. AT ALL TIMES.
AND THAT'S WHY I'M HERE TODAY. FOR YOUR SON. I'M GONNA MAKE HIM A STAR.
HIS HARD WORK AND DEDICATION WILL MAKE HIM A STAR, MR TALBOT.
9
ABSOLUTELY...
ABSOLUTELY.
AND HE'S GOT A CONTRACT ALREADY. WITH MELCHESTER ROVERS. THANK YOU.
A ROLLING WEEK-TO-WEEK CONTRACT. IN LEAGUE TWO? I TAKE IT YOU DID NOT HAVE REPRESENTATION WHEN YOU AGREED TO THAT?
UH... NO.
SON, I SAW WHAT YOU DID AGAINST TYNECASTER IN THE FA CUP. THAT GOAL. AND YOU ALMOST WON IT IN THE LAST FEW MINUTES THERE. PLAYING AGAINST GALACTICOS!
YOU WANT TO BE IN THE TOP FLIGHT, YEAH? EUROPE? PLAY FOR ENGLAND? ALL THAT.
YEAH.
AND THAT'S WHERE YOU SHOULD BE. JUMP IN, I'LL DRIVE YOU TO THE GROUND. SAVE YOUR LEGS FOR THE GAME. WE CAN HAVE A LITTLE CHAT.

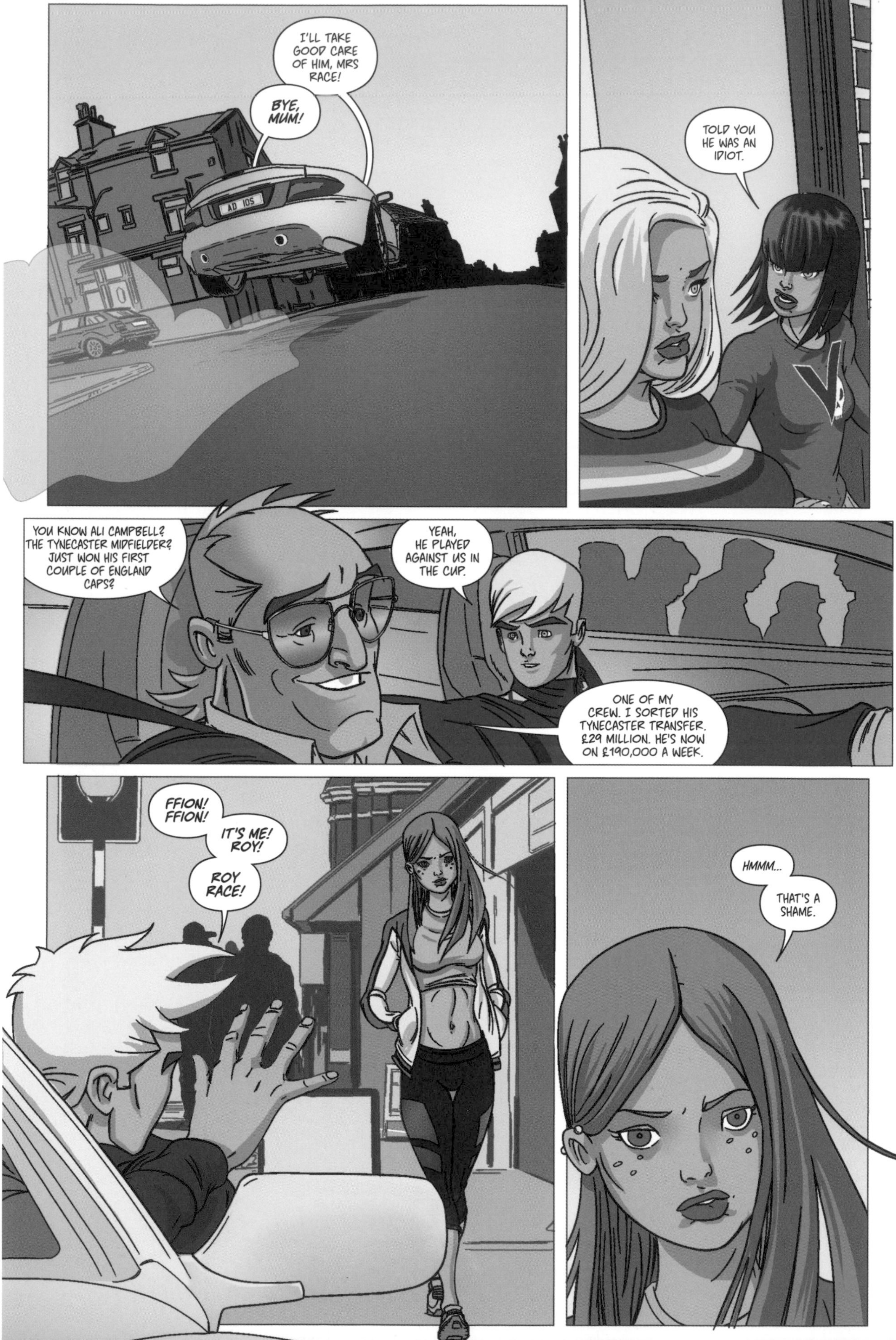
I'LL TAKE GOOD CARE OF HIM, MRS RACE!
BYE, MUM!
AD 10S
TOLD YOU HE WAS AN IDIOT.
YOU KNOW ALI CAMPBELL? THE TYNECASTER MIDFIELDER? JUST WON HIS FIRST COUPLE OF ENGLAND CAPS?
YEAH, HE PLAYED AGAINST US IN THE CUP.
ONE OF MY CREW. I SORTED HIS TYNECASTER TRANSFER. £29 MILLION. HE'S NOW ON £190,000 A WEEK.
FFION! FFION!
IT'S ME! ROY!
ROY RACE!
HMMM...
THAT'S A SHAME.

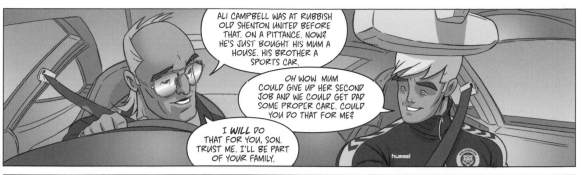

ALI CAMPBELL WAS AT RUBBISH OLD SHENTON UNITED BEFORE THAT. ON A PITTANCE. NOW? HE'S JUST BOUGHT HIS MUM A HOUSE. HIS BROTHER A SPORTS CAR.

OH WOW MUM COULD GIVE UP HER SECOND JOB AND WE COULD GET DAD SOME PROPER CARE. COULD YOU DO THAT FOR ME?

I *WILL* DO THAT FOR YOU, SON. TRUST ME. I'LL BE PART OF YOUR FAMILY.

IF YOU CAN PROVE WHAT YOU DID AGAINST TYNECASTER WASN'T A FLASH IN THE PAN, ROD.

...ROY...

PLAYERS ENTRANCE

I'M GOING TO BE WATCHING YOU, ROY.

KEEP KNOCKING THEM IN AND I'LL MAKE SURE YOU'RE NOT SLUMMING IT DOWN HERE WITH THESE LOSERS MUCH LONGER.

THEY'RE SELLING THE GROUND SOON YOU KNOW.

I'M NOT SLUMMIN...

SKREEEEEEEEEEE!!!

...WHAT DID YOU SAY ABOUT THE GROUND?

I DON'T THINK THAT...

YOU'RE NOT... I MEAN, WE'RE NOT...

REALLY.

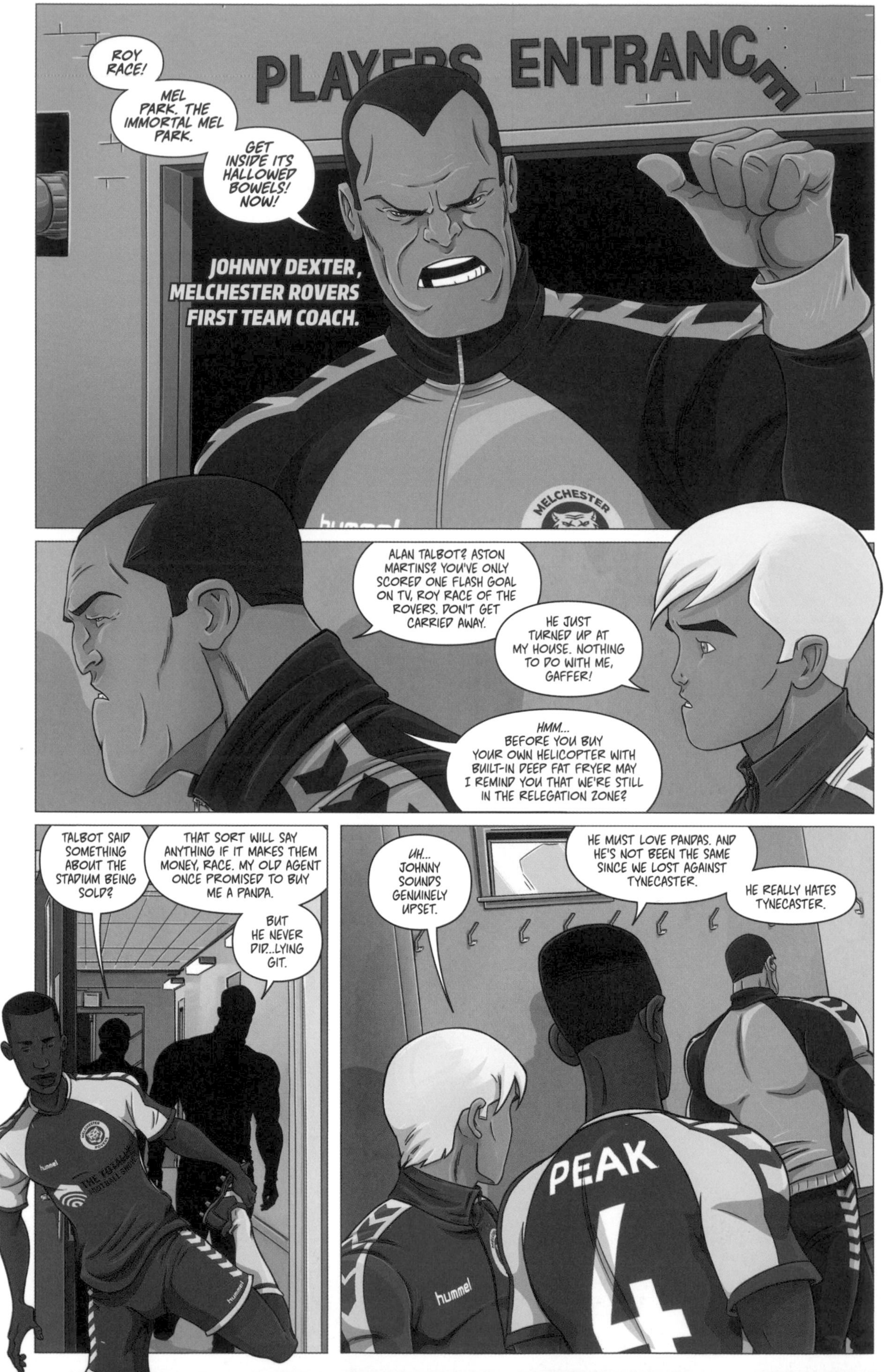
PLAYERS ENTRANCE
ROY RACE!
MEL PARK. THE IMMORTAL MEL PARK.
GET INSIDE ITS HALLOWED BOWELS! NOW!
JOHNNY DEXTER, MELCHESTER ROVERS FIRST TEAM COACH.
MELCHESTER
hummel
ALAN TALBOT? ASTON MARTINS? YOU'VE ONLY SCORED ONE FLASH GOAL ON TV, ROY RACE OF THE ROVERS. DON'T GET CARRIED AWAY.
HE JUST TURNED UP AT MY HOUSE. NOTHING TO DO WITH ME, GAFFER!
HMM... BEFORE YOU BUY YOUR OWN HELICOPTER WITH BUILT-IN DEEP FAT FRYER MAY I REMIND YOU THAT WE'RE STILL IN THE RELEGATION ZONE?
TALBOT SAID SOMETHING ABOUT THE STADIUM BEING SOLD?
THAT SORT WILL SAY ANYTHING IF IT MAKES THEM MONEY, RACE. MY OLD AGENT ONCE PROMISED TO BUY ME A PANDA.
BUT HE NEVER DID...LYING GIT.
hummel
UH... JOHNNY SOUNDS GENUINELY UPSET.
HE MUST LOVE PANDAS. AND HE'S NOT BEEN THE SAME SINCE WE LOST AGAINST TYNECASTER.
HE REALLY HATES TYNECASTER.
PEAK
4
hummel

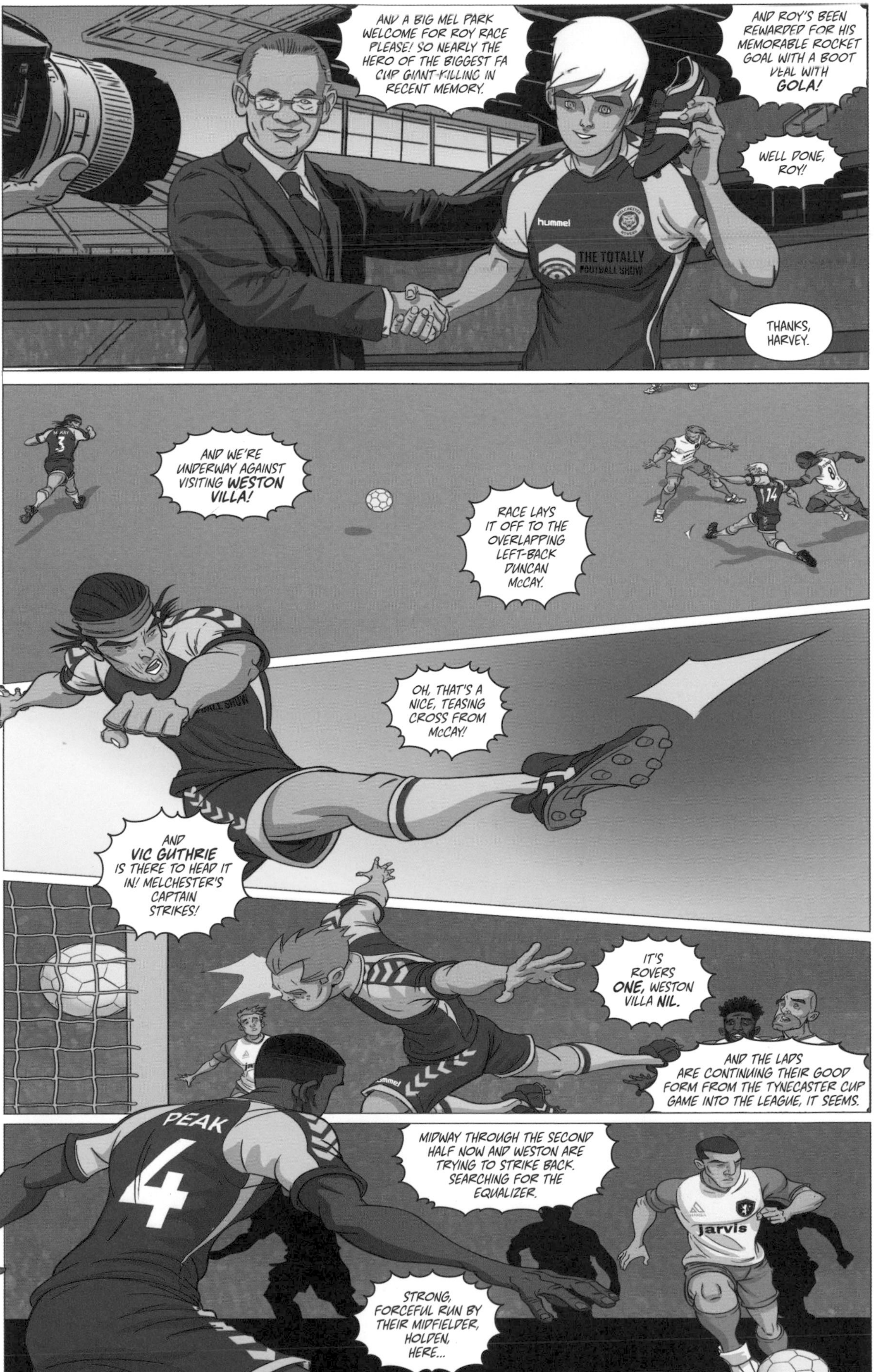
AND A BIG MEL PARK WELCOME FOR ROY RACE PLEASE! SO NEARLY THE HERO OF THE BIGGEST FA CUP GIANT-KILLING IN RECENT MEMORY.
AND ROY'S BEEN REWARDED FOR HIS MEMORABLE ROCKET GOAL WITH A BOOT DEAL WITH GOLA!
WELL DONE, ROY!
THANKS, HARVEY.
AND WE'RE UNDERWAY AGAINST VISITING WESTON VILLA!
RACE LAYS IT OFF TO THE OVERLAPPING LEFT-BACK DUNCAN McCAY.
OH, THAT'S A NICE, TEASING CROSS FROM McCAY!
AND VIC GUTHRIE IS THERE TO HEAD IT IN! MELCHESTER'S CAPTAIN STRIKES!
IT'S ROVERS ONE, WESTON VILLA NIL.
AND THE LADS ARE CONTINUING THEIR GOOD FORM FROM THE TYNECASTER CUP GAME INTO THE LEAGUE, IT SEEMS.
PEAK
4
MIDWAY THROUGH THE SECOND HALF NOW AND WESTON ARE TRYING TO STRIKE BACK. SEARCHING FOR THE EQUALIZER.
jarvis
STRONG, FORCEFUL RUN BY THEIR MIDFIELDER, HOLDEN, HERE...

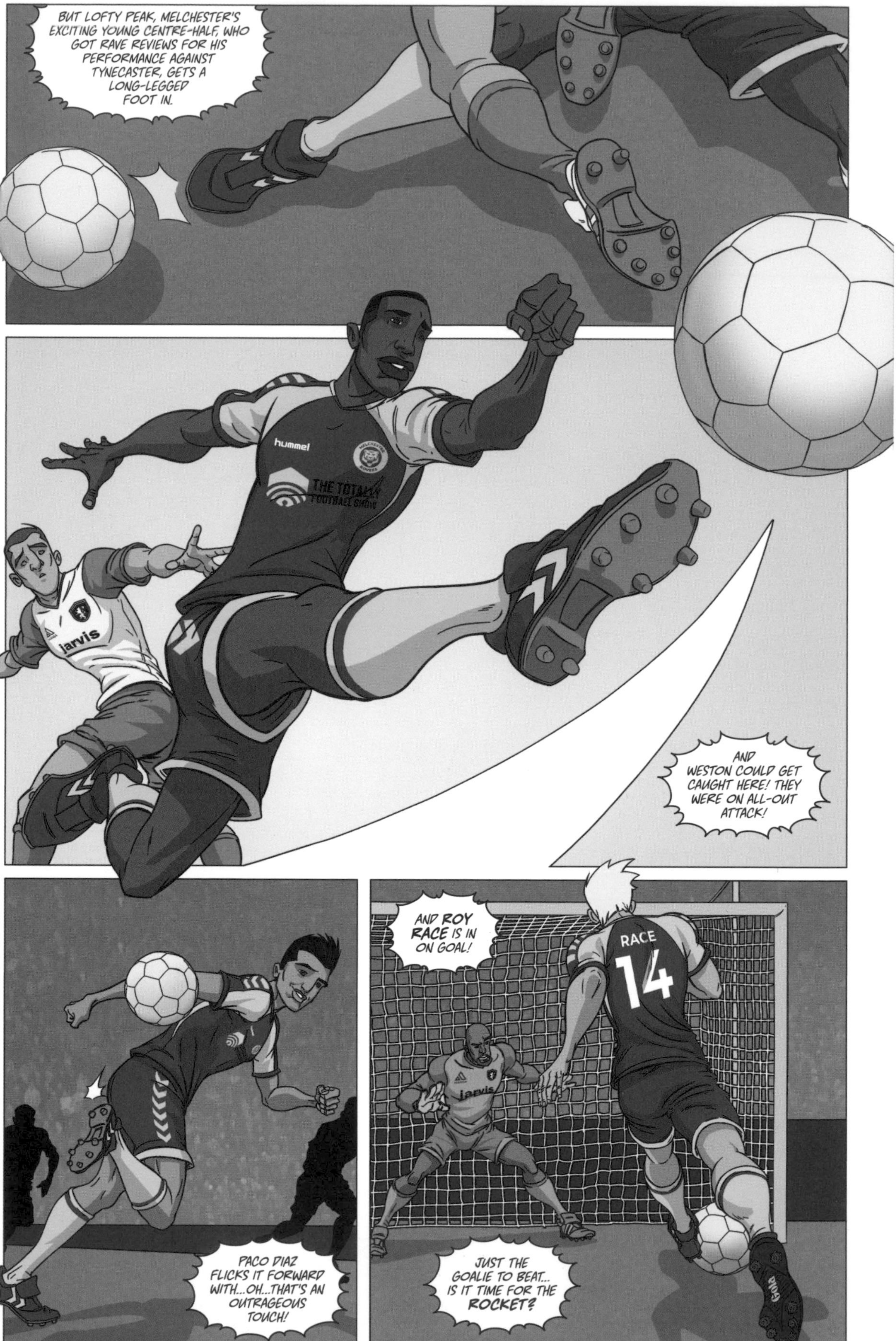
BUT LOFTY PEAK, MELCHESTER'S EXCITING YOUNG CENTRE-HALF, WHO GOT RAVE REVIEWS FOR HIS PERFORMANCE AGAINST TYNECASTER, GETS A LONG-LEGGED FOOT IN.
hummel
THE TOTALLY FOOTBALL SHOW
jarvis
AND WESTON COULD GET CAUGHT HERE! THEY WERE ON ALL-OUT ATTACK!
PACO DIAZ FLICKS IT FORWARD WITH...OH...THAT'S AN OUTRAGEOUS TOUCH!
AND ROY RACE IS IN ON GOAL!
RACE
14
jarvis
JUST THE GOALIE TO BEAT... IS IT TIME FOR THE ROCKET?

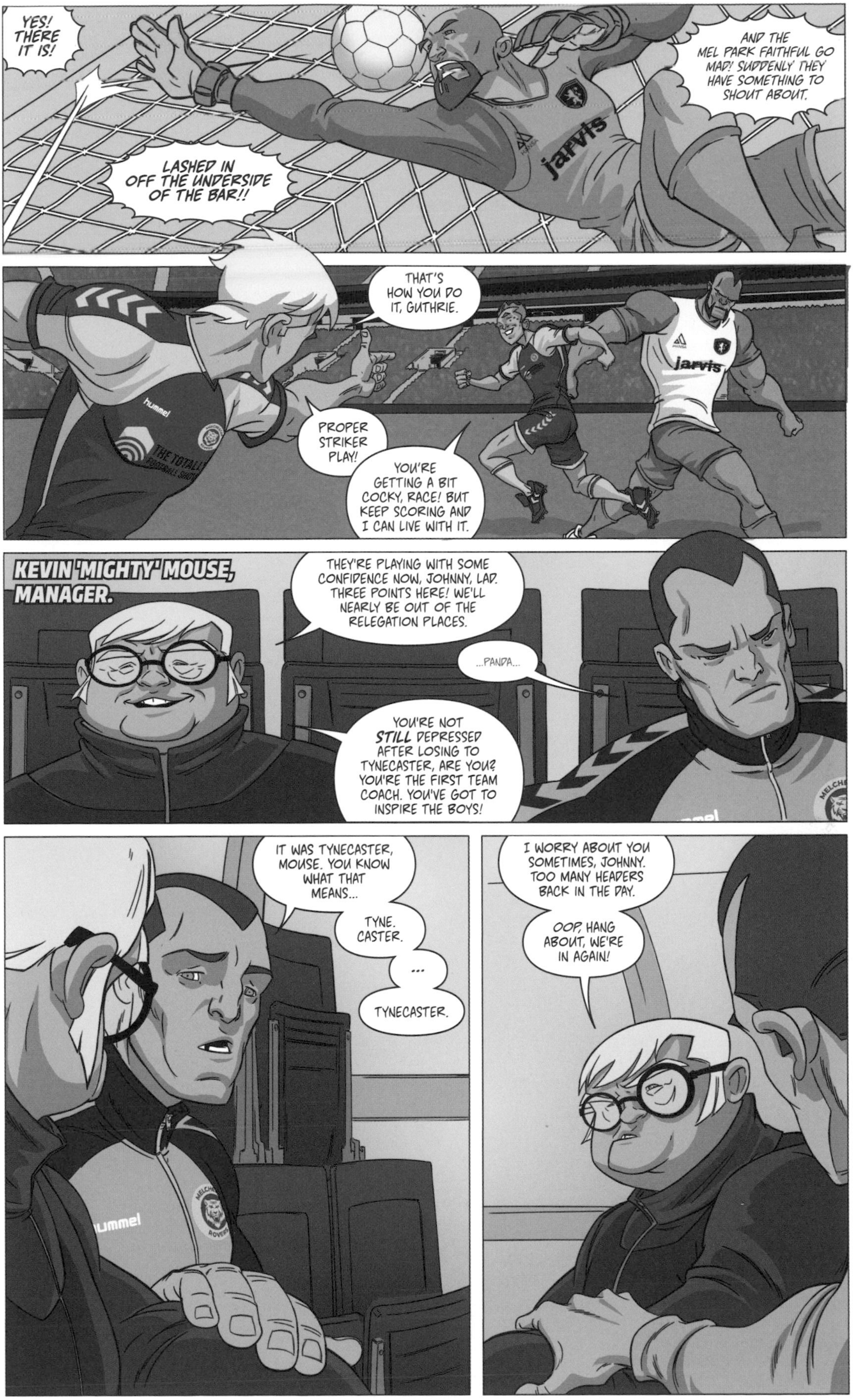
YES! THERE IT IS!
AND THE MEL PARK FAITHFUL GO MAD! SUDDENLY THEY HAVE SOMETHING TO SHOUT ABOUT.
LASHED IN OFF THE UNDERSIDE OF THE BAR!!
THAT'S HOW YOU DO IT, GUTHRIE.
PROPER STRIKER PLAY!
YOU'RE GETTING A BIT COCKY, RACE! BUT KEEP SCORING AND I CAN LIVE WITH IT.
KEVIN 'MIGHTY' MOUSE, MANAGER.
THEY'RE PLAYING WITH SOME CONFIDENCE NOW, JOHNNY, LAD. THREE POINTS HERE! WE'LL NEARLY BE OUT OF THE RELEGATION PLACES.
...PANDA...
YOU'RE NOT STILL DEPRESSED AFTER LOSING TO TYNECASTER, ARE YOU? YOU'RE THE FIRST TEAM COACH. YOU'VE GOT TO INSPIRE THE BOYS!
IT WAS TYNECASTER, MOUSE. YOU KNOW WHAT THAT MEANS...
TYNE. CASTER.
...
TYNECASTER.
I WORRY ABOUT YOU SOMETIMES, JOHNNY. TOO MANY HEADERS BACK IN THE DAY.
OOP, HANG ABOUT, WE'RE IN AGAIN!

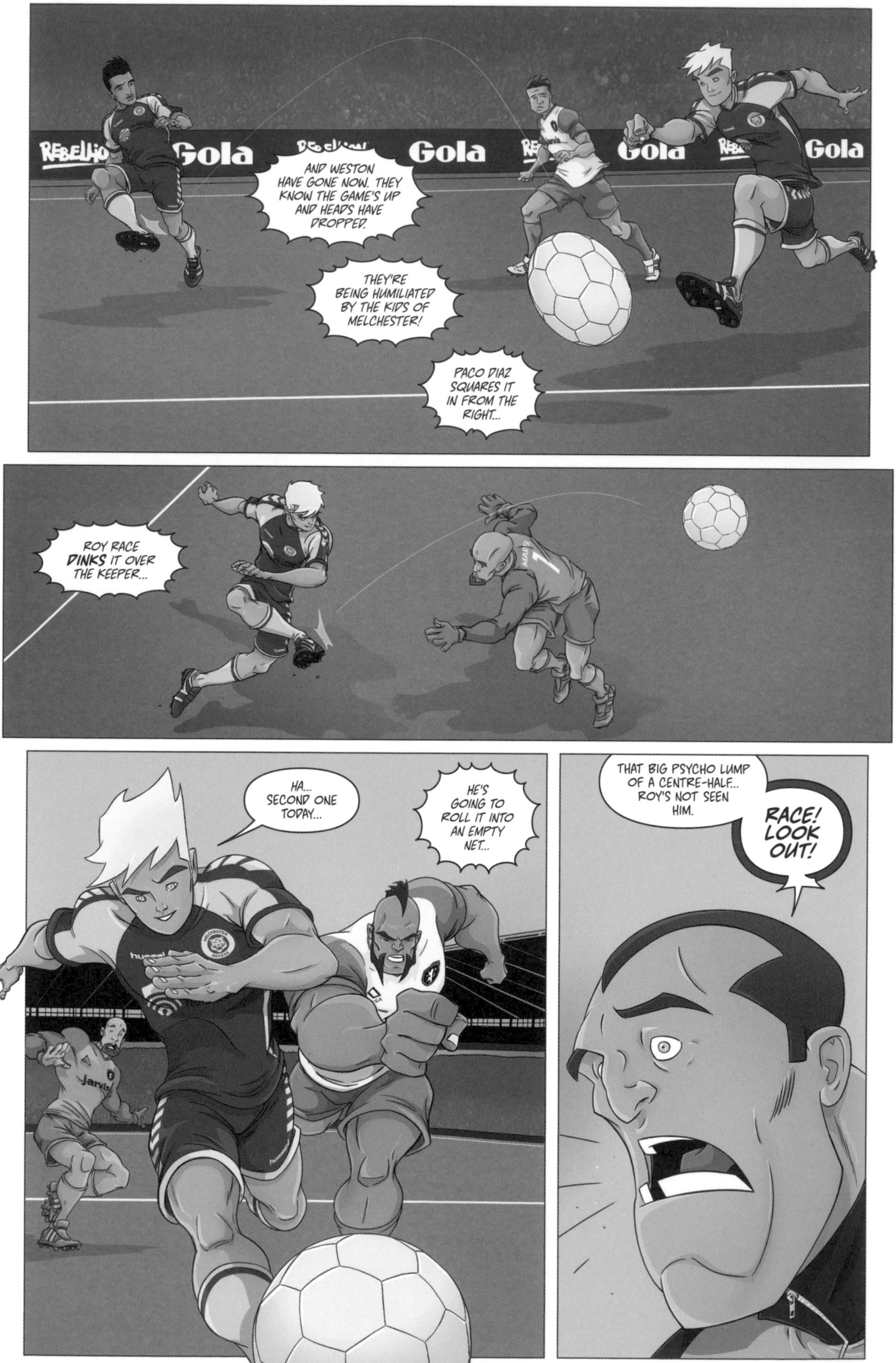
AND WESTON HAVE GONE NOW. THEY KNOW THE GAME'S UP AND HEADS HAVE DROPPED.
THEY'RE BEING HUMILIATED BY THE KIDS OF MELCHESTER!
PACO DIAZ SQUARES IT IN FROM THE RIGHT...
ROY RACE **DINKS** IT OVER THE KEEPER...
HA... SECOND ONE TODAY...
HE'S GOING TO ROLL IT INTO AN EMPTY NET...
THAT BIG PSYCHO LUMP OF A CENTRE-HALF... ROY'S NOT SEEN HIM.
RACE! LOOK OUT!

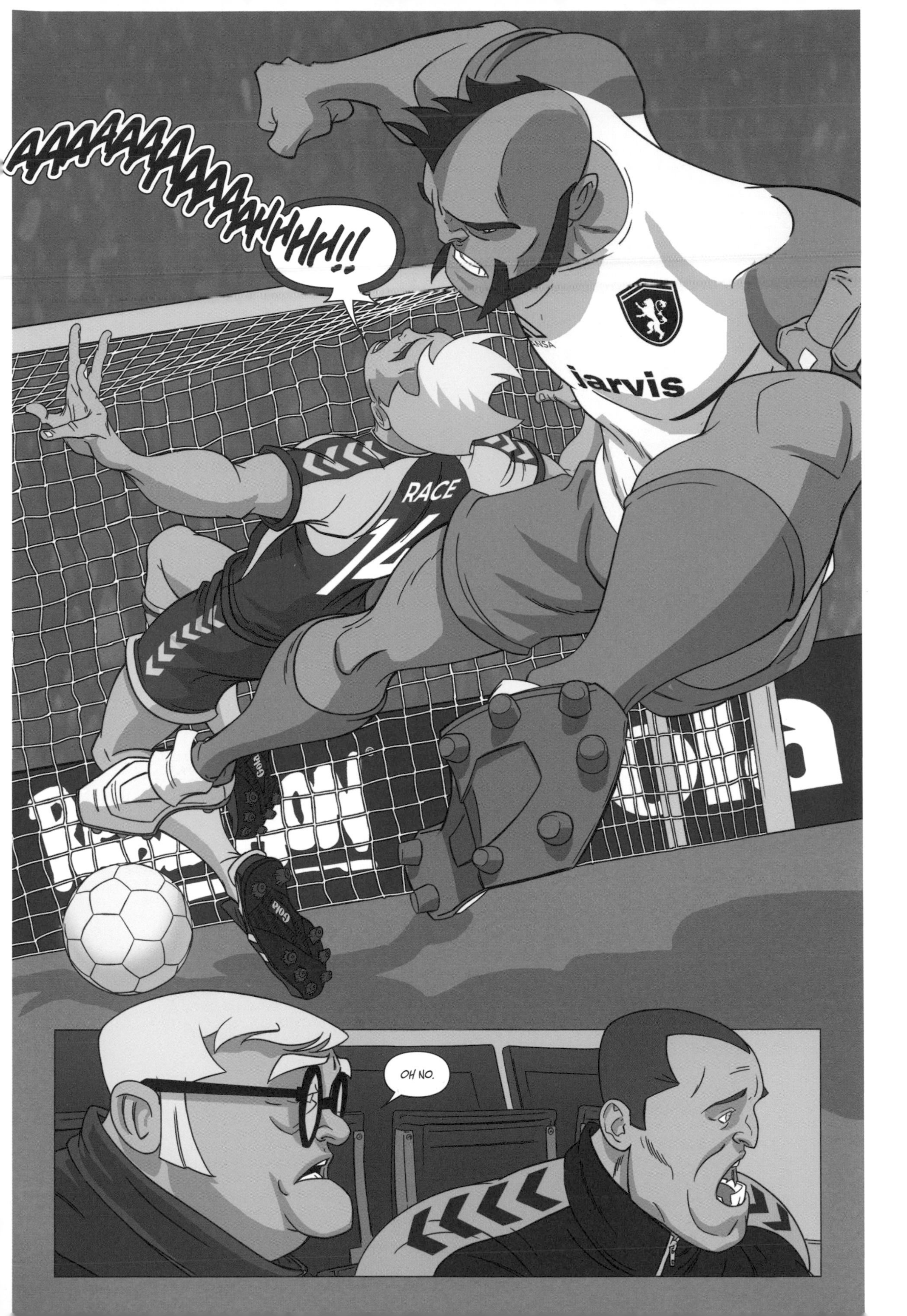
AAAAAAAAAAAAAAHHHH!!
RACE
Jarvis
OH NO.

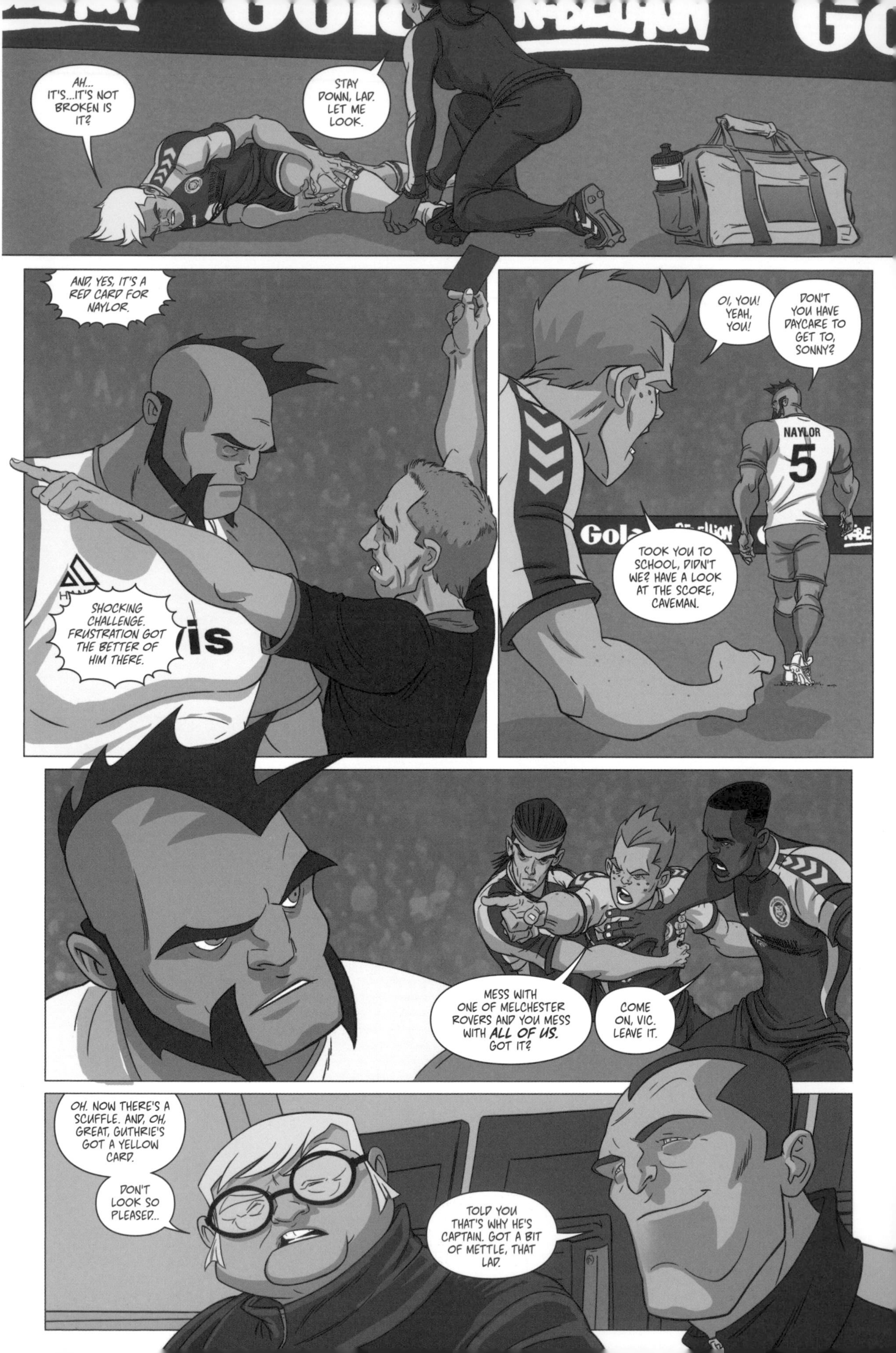
AH... IT'S...IT'S NOT BROKEN IS IT?
STAY DOWN, LAD. LET ME LOOK.
AND, YES, IT'S A RED CARD FOR NAYLOR.
SHOCKING CHALLENGE. FRUSTRATION GOT THE BETTER OF HIM THERE.
OI, YOU! YEAH, YOU!
DON'T YOU HAVE DAYCARE TO GET TO, SONNY?
NAYLOR
5
TOOK YOU TO SCHOOL, DIDN'T WE? HAVE A LOOK AT THE SCORE, CAVEMAN.
MESS WITH ONE OF MELCHESTER ROVERS AND YOU MESS WITH ALL OF US. GOT IT?
COME ON, VIC. LEAVE IT.
OH. NOW THERE'S A SCUFFLE. AND, OH, GREAT, GUTHRIE'S GOT A YELLOW CARD.
DON'T LOOK SO PLEASED...
TOLD YOU THAT'S WHY HE'S CAPTAIN. GOT A BIT OF METTLE, THAT LAD.

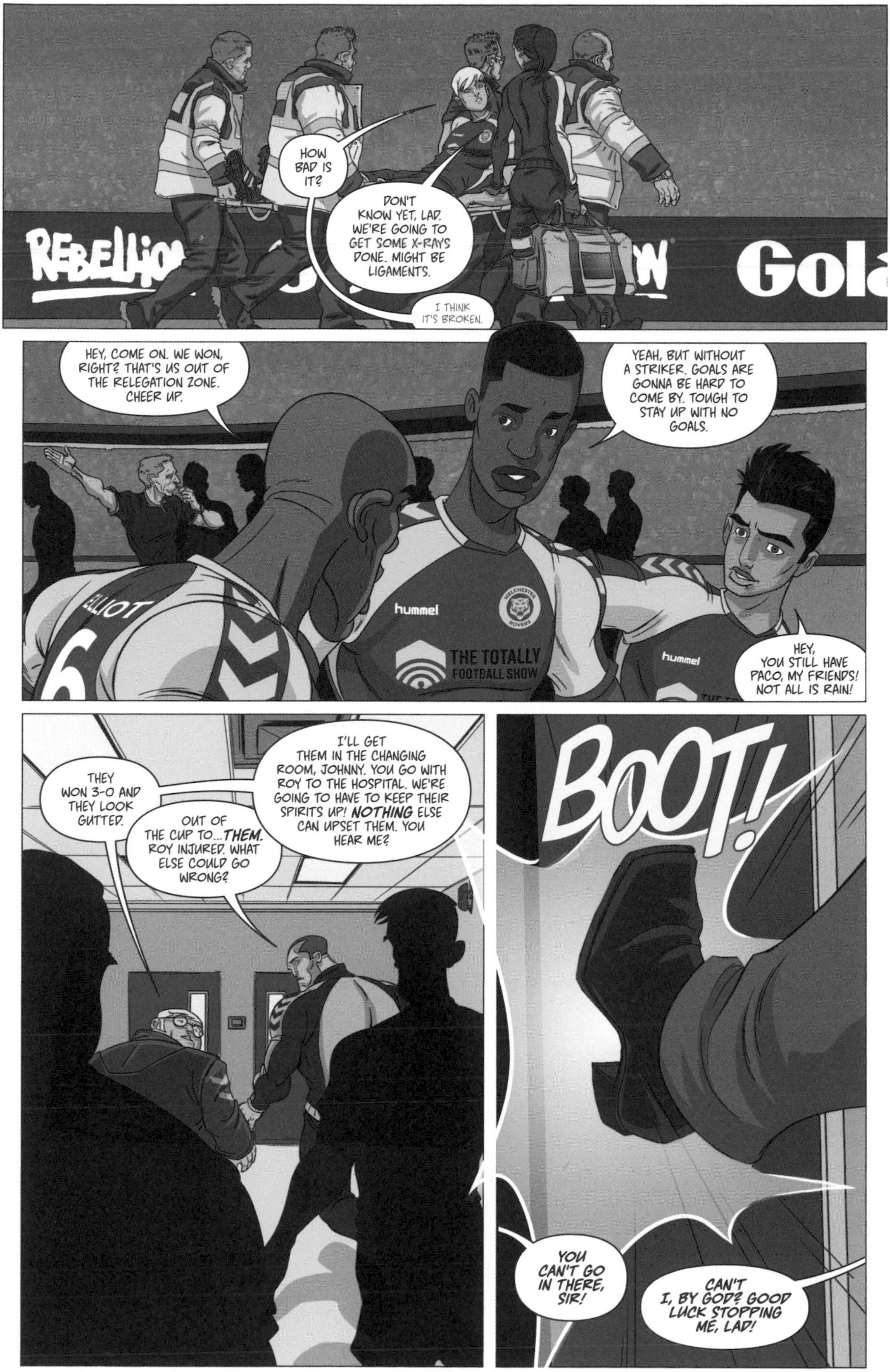
HOW BAD IS IT?
DON'T KNOW YET, LAD. WE'RE GOING TO GET SOME X-RAYS DONE. MIGHT BE LIGAMENTS.
I THINK IT'S BROKEN.
HEY, COME ON. WE WON, RIGHT? THAT'S US OUT OF THE RELEGATION ZONE. CHEER UP.
YEAH, BUT WITHOUT A STRIKER. GOALS ARE GONNA BE HARD TO COME BY. TOUGH TO STAY UP WITH NO GOALS.
ELLIOT
6
hummel
THE TOTALLY FOOTBALL SHOW
HEY, YOU STILL HAVE PACO, MY FRIENDS! NOT ALL IS RAIN!
THEY WON 3-0 AND THEY LOOK GUTTED.
OUT OF THE CUP TO... ***THEM.*** ROY INJURED. WHAT ELSE COULD GO WRONG?
I'LL GET THEM IN THE CHANGING ROOM, JOHNNY. YOU GO WITH ROY TO THE HOSPITAL. WE'RE GOING TO HAVE TO KEEP THEIR SPIRITS UP! ***NOTHING*** ELSE CAN UPSET THEM. YOU HEAR ME?
BOOT!
YOU CAN'T GO IN THERE, SIR!
CAN'T I, BY GOD? GOOD LUCK STOPPING ME, LAD!

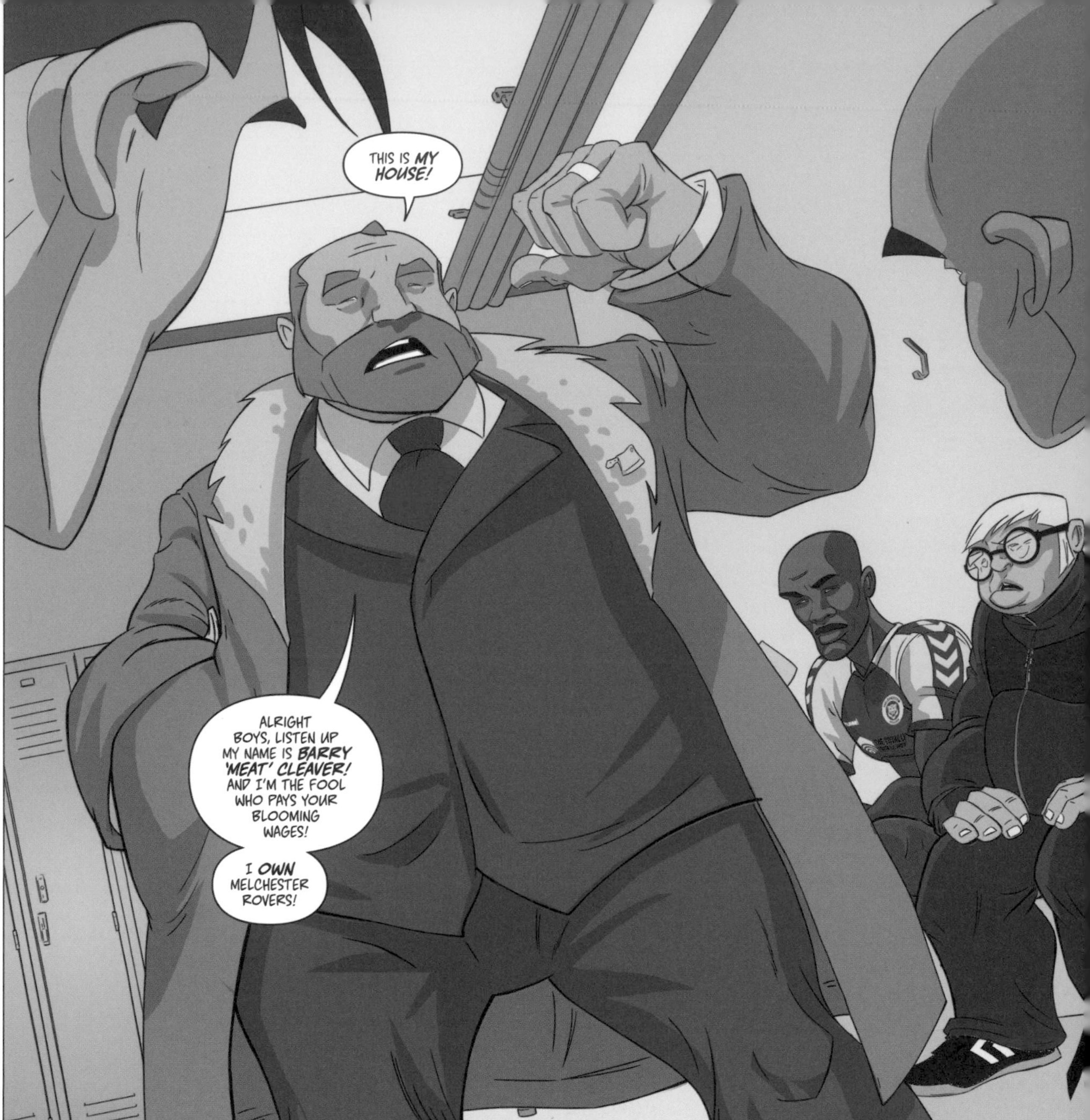
THIS IS MY HOUSE!
ALRIGHT BOYS, LISTEN UP MY NAME IS BARRY 'MEAT' CLEAVER! AND I'M THE FOOL WHO PAYS YOUR BLOOMING WAGES!
I OWN MELCHESTER ROVERS!

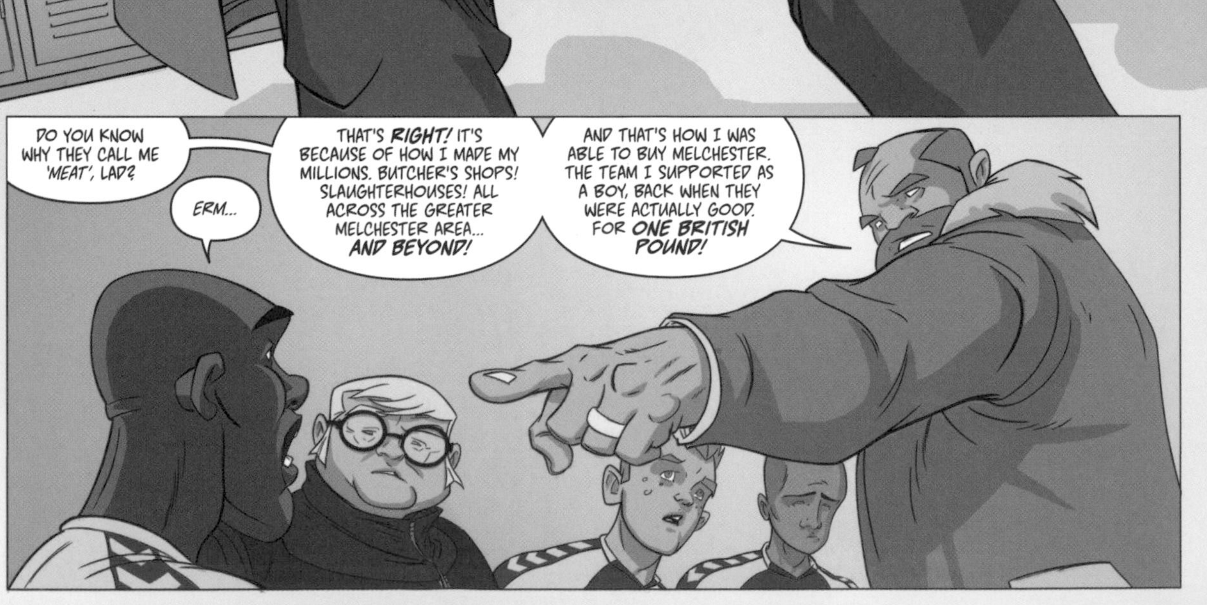
DO YOU KNOW WHY THEY CALL ME 'MEAT', LAD?
ERM...
THAT'S RIGHT! IT'S BECAUSE OF HOW I MADE MY MILLIONS. BUTCHER'S SHOPS! SLAUGHTERHOUSES! ALL ACROSS THE GREATER MELCHESTER AREA... AND BEYOND!
AND THAT'S HOW I WAS ABLE TO BUY MELCHESTER. THE TEAM I SUPPORTED AS A BOY, BACK WHEN THEY WERE ACTUALLY GOOD. FOR ONE BRITISH POUND!

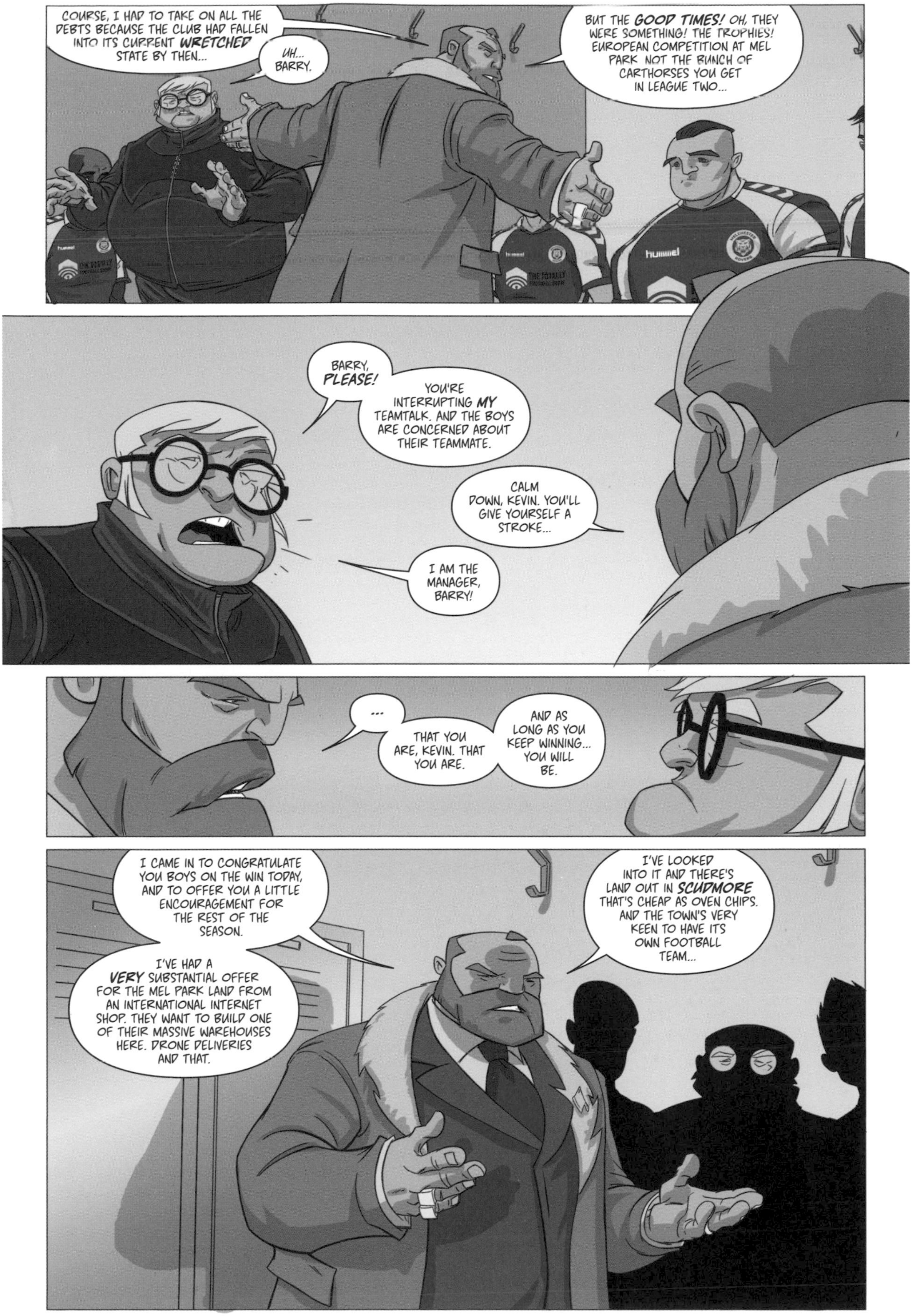
COURSE, I HAD TO TAKE ON ALL THE DEBTS BECAUSE THE CLUB HAD FALLEN INTO ITS CURRENT WRETCHED STATE BY THEN...
UH... BARRY.
BUT THE GOOD TIMES! OH, THEY WERE SOMETHING! THE TROPHIES! EUROPEAN COMPETITION AT MEL PARK NOT THE BUNCH OF CARTHORSES YOU GET IN LEAGUE TWO...
hummel
BARRY, PLEASE!
YOU'RE INTERRUPTING MY TEAMTALK. AND THE BOYS ARE CONCERNED ABOUT THEIR TEAMMATE.
CALM DOWN, KEVIN. YOU'LL GIVE YOURSELF A STROKE...
I AM THE MANAGER, BARRY!
...
THAT YOU ARE, KEVIN. THAT YOU ARE.
AND AS LONG AS YOU KEEP WINNING... YOU WILL BE.
I CAME IN TO CONGRATULATE YOU BOYS ON THE WIN TODAY, AND TO OFFER YOU A LITTLE ENCOURAGEMENT FOR THE REST OF THE SEASON.
I'VE HAD A VERY SUBSTANTIAL OFFER FOR THE MEL PARK LAND FROM AN INTERNATIONAL INTERNET SHOP. THEY WANT TO BUILD ONE OF THEIR MASSIVE WAREHOUSES HERE. DRONE DELIVERIES AND THAT.
I'VE LOOKED INTO IT AND THERE'S LAND OUT IN SCUDMORE THAT'S CHEAP AS OVEN CHIPS. AND THE TOWN'S VERY KEEN TO HAVE ITS OWN FOOTBALL TEAM...

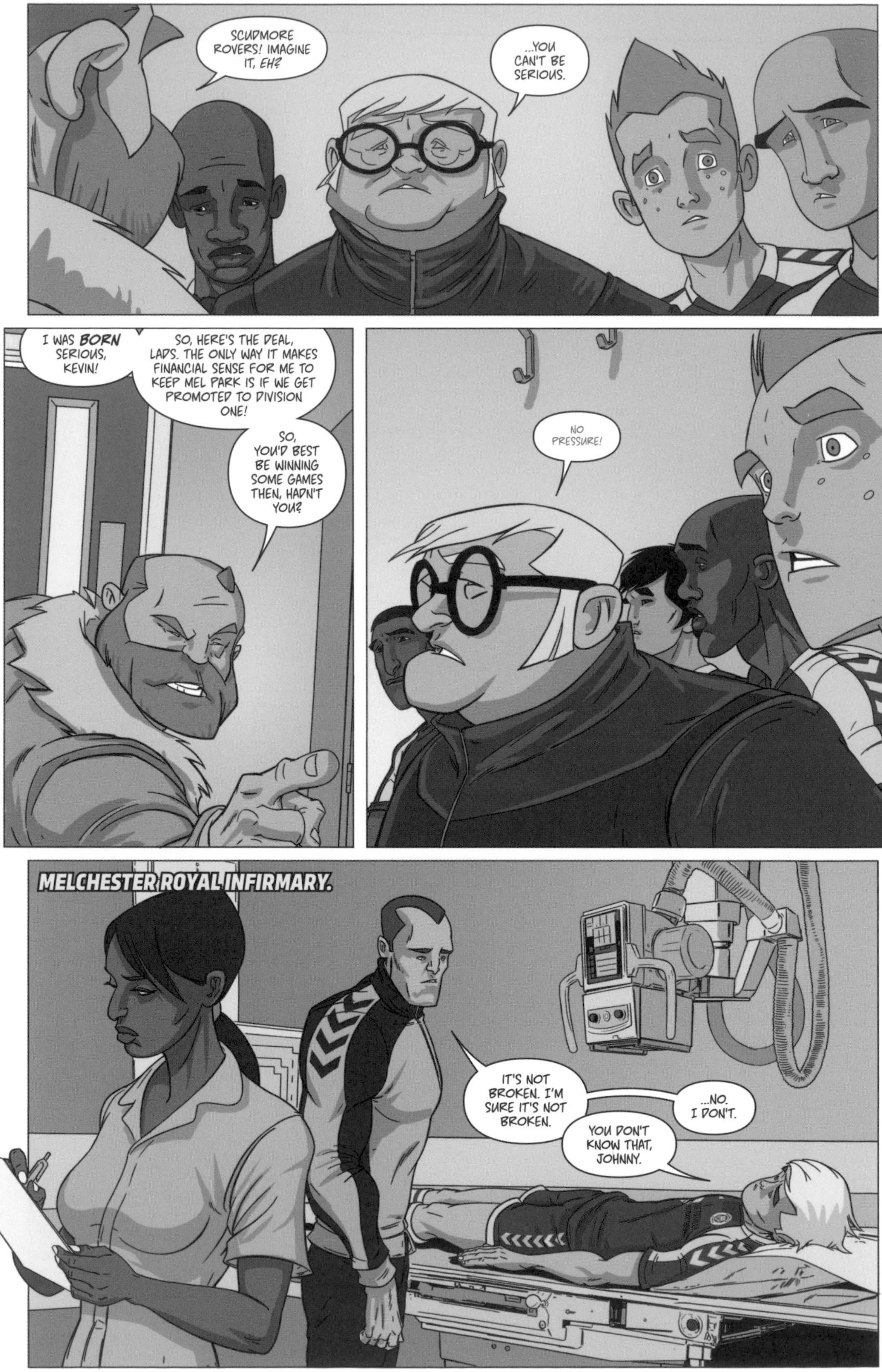
SCUDMORE ROVERS! IMAGINE IT, EH?
...YOU CAN'T BE SERIOUS.
I WAS BORN SERIOUS, KEVIN!
SO, HERE'S THE DEAL, LADS. THE ONLY WAY IT MAKES FINANCIAL SENSE FOR ME TO KEEP MEL PARK IS IF WE GET PROMOTED TO DIVISION ONE!
SO, YOU'D BEST BE WINNING SOME GAMES THEN, HADN'T YOU?
NO PRESSURE!
MELCHESTER ROYAL INFIRMARY.
IT'S NOT BROKEN. I'M SURE IT'S NOT BROKEN.
YOU DON'T KNOW THAT, JOHNNY.
...NO. I DON'T.

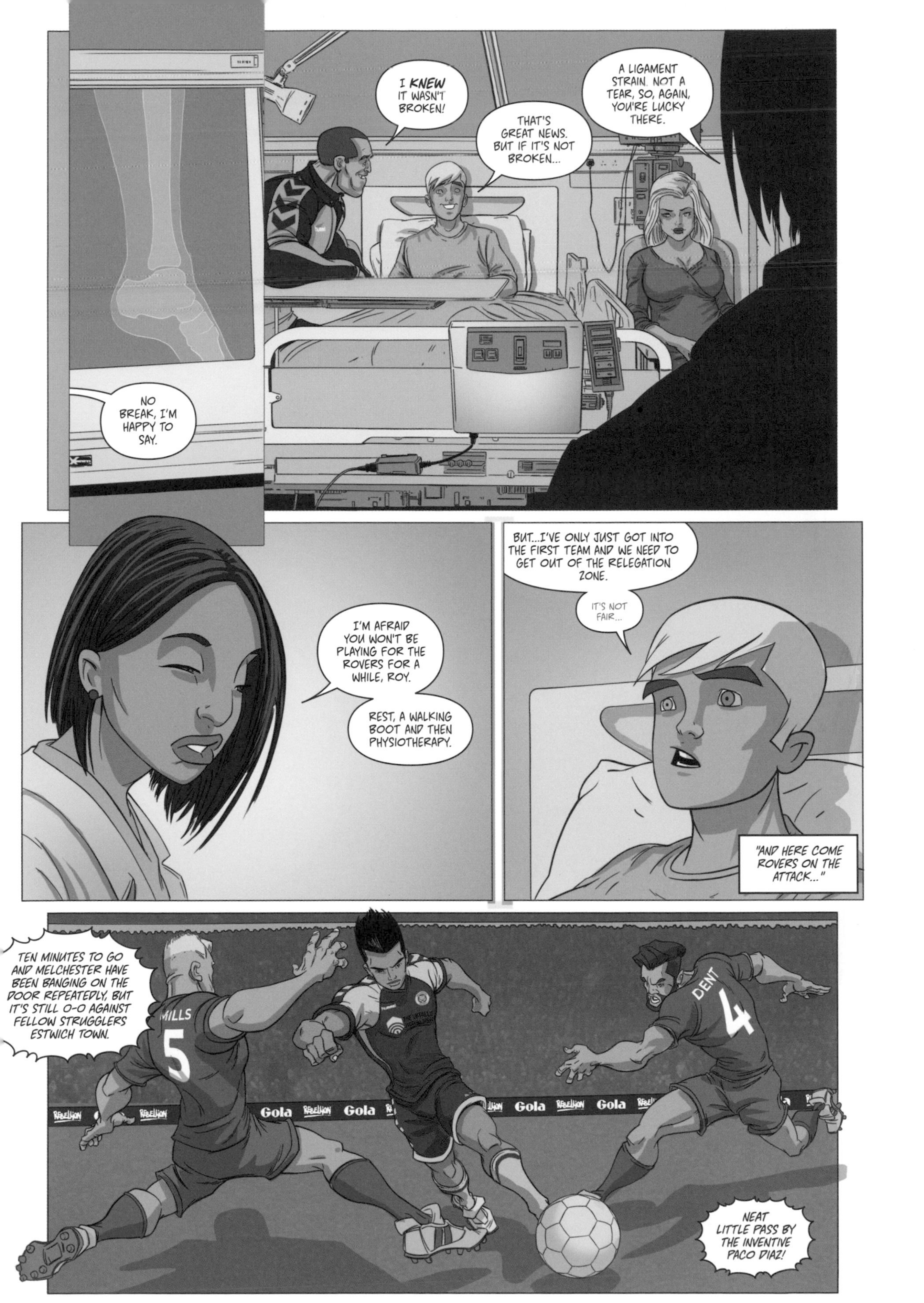
I KNEW IT WASN'T BROKEN!
THAT'S GREAT NEWS. BUT IF IT'S NOT BROKEN...
A LIGAMENT STRAIN. NOT A TEAR, SO, AGAIN, YOU'RE LUCKY THERE.
NO BREAK, I'M HAPPY TO SAY.
I'M AFRAID YOU WON'T BE PLAYING FOR THE ROVERS FOR A WHILE, ROY.
REST, A WALKING BOOT AND THEN PHYSIOTHERAPY.
BUT...I'VE ONLY JUST GOT INTO THE FIRST TEAM AND WE NEED TO GET OUT OF THE RELEGATION ZONE.
IT'S NOT FAIR...
"AND HERE COME ROVERS ON THE ATTACK..."
TEN MINUTES TO GO AND MELCHESTER HAVE BEEN BANGING ON THE DOOR REPEATEDLY, BUT IT'S STILL 0-0 AGAINST FELLOW STRUGGLERS ESTWICH TOWN.
MILLS 5
DENT 4
Gola
REBELLION
NEAT LITTLE PASS BY THE INVENTIVE PACO DIAZ!

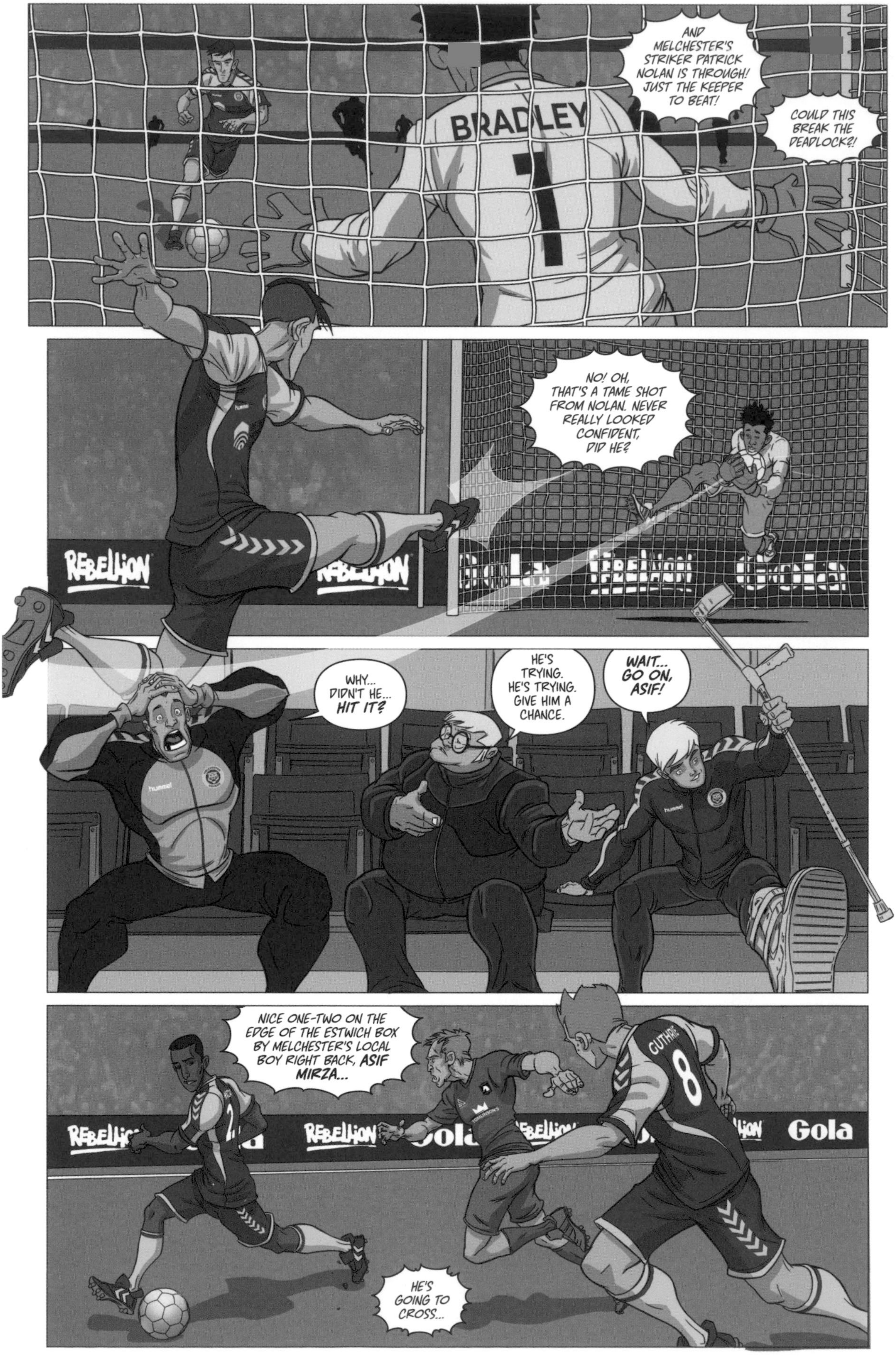
BRADLEY
AND MELCHESTER'S STRIKER PATRICK NOLAN IS THROUGH! JUST THE KEEPER TO BEAT!
COULD THIS BREAK THE DEADLOCK?!
REBELLION
NO! OH, THAT'S A TAME SHOT FROM NOLAN. NEVER REALLY LOOKED CONFIDENT, DID HE?
WHY... DIDN'T HE... **HIT IT?**
HE'S TRYING. HE'S TRYING. GIVE HIM A CHANCE.
WAIT... GO ON, ASIF!
NICE ONE-TWO ON THE EDGE OF THE ESTWICH BOX BY MELCHESTER'S LOCAL BOY RIGHT BACK, **ASIF MIRZA...**
REBELLION
Gola
GUTHRIE
HE'S GOING TO CROSS...

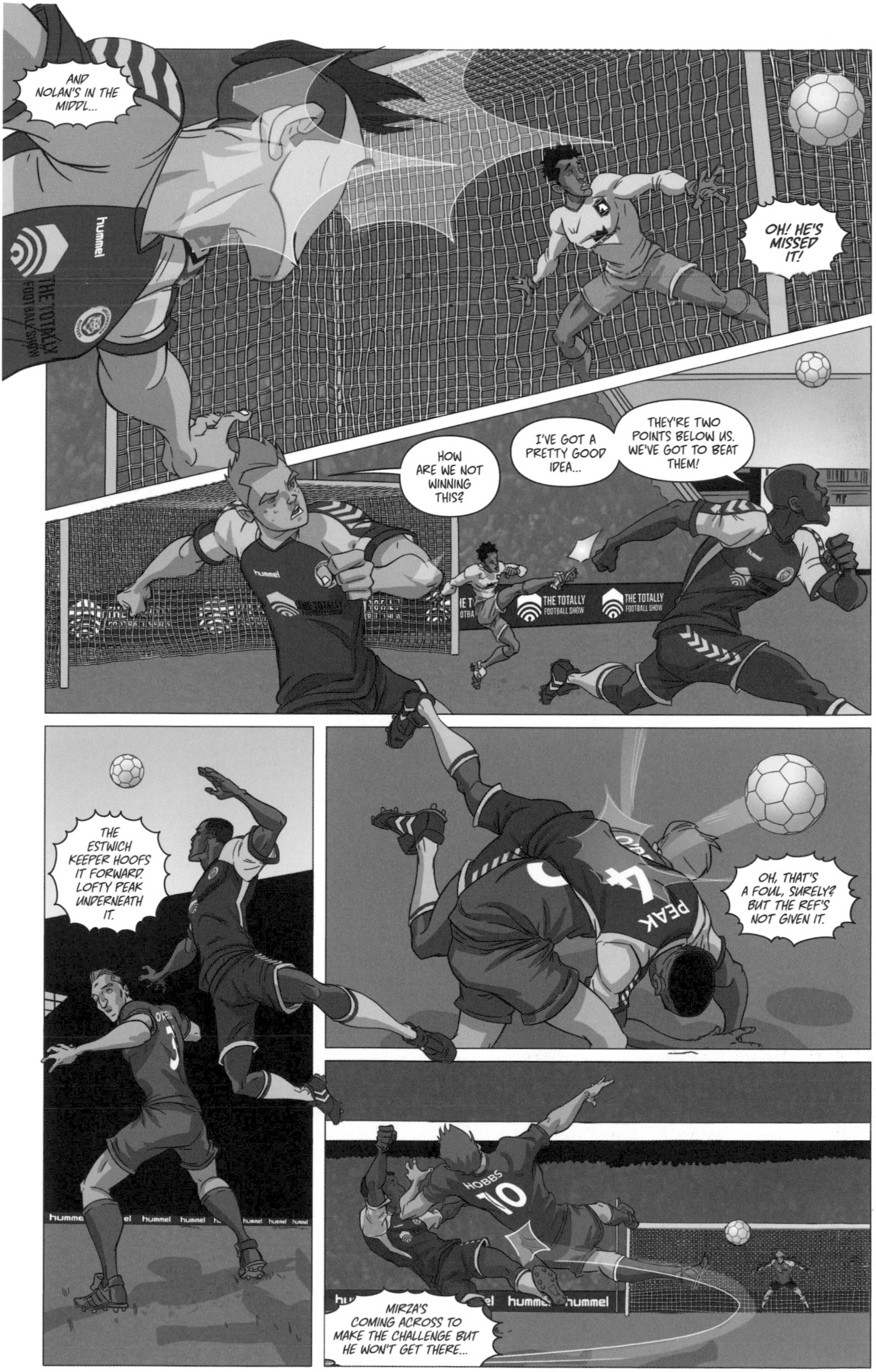
AND NOLAN'S IN THE MIDDL...
OH! HE'S MISSED IT!
hummel
THE TOTALLY FOOTBALL SHOW
HOW ARE WE NOT WINNING THIS?
I'VE GOT A PRETTY GOOD IDEA...
THEY'RE TWO POINTS BELOW US. WE'VE GOT TO BEAT THEM!
THE TOTALLY FOOTBALL SHOW
THE ESTWICH KEEPER HOOFS IT FORWARD. LOFTY PEAK UNDERNEATH IT.
PEAK
4
OH, THAT'S A FOUL, SURELY? BUT THE REF'S NOT GIVEN IT.
HOBBS
10
MIRZA'S COMING ACROSS TO MAKE THE CHALLENGE BUT HE WON'T GET THERE...

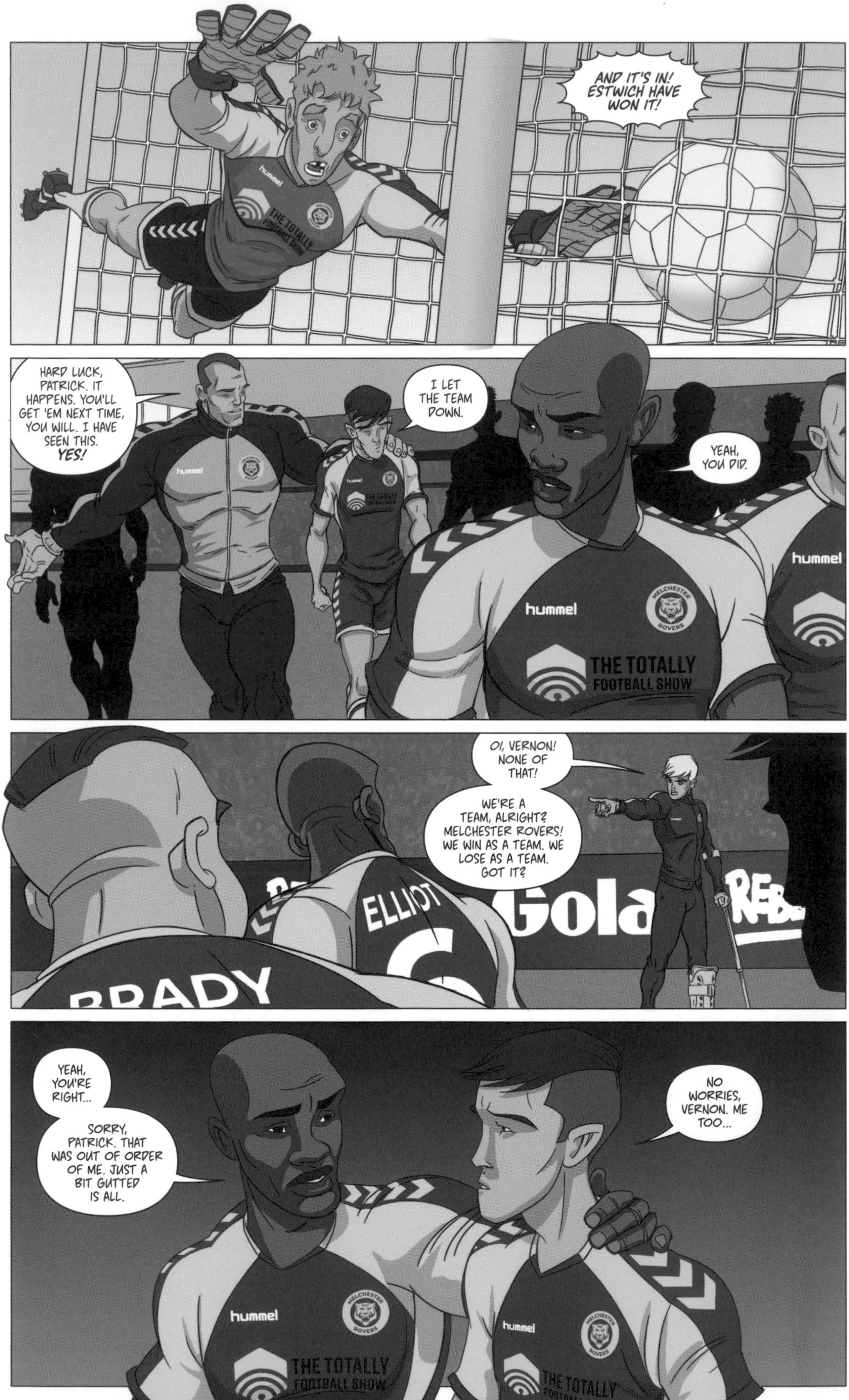
AND IT'S IN! ESTWICH HAVE WON IT!
hummel
THE TOTALLY FOOTBALL SHOW
HARD LUCK, PATRICK. IT HAPPENS. YOU'LL GET 'EM NEXT TIME, YOU WILL. I HAVE SEEN THIS. **YES!**
I LET THE TEAM DOWN.
YEAH, YOU DID.
hummel
MELCHESTER ROVERS
THE TOTALLY FOOTBALL SHOW
OI, VERNON! NONE OF THAT!
WE'RE A TEAM, ALRIGHT? MELCHESTER ROVERS! WE WIN AS A TEAM. WE LOSE AS A TEAM. GOT IT?
ELLIOT
BRADY
YEAH, YOU'RE RIGHT...
SORRY, PATRICK. THAT WAS OUT OF ORDER OF ME. JUST A BIT GUTTED IS ALL.
NO WORRIES, VERNON. ME TOO...

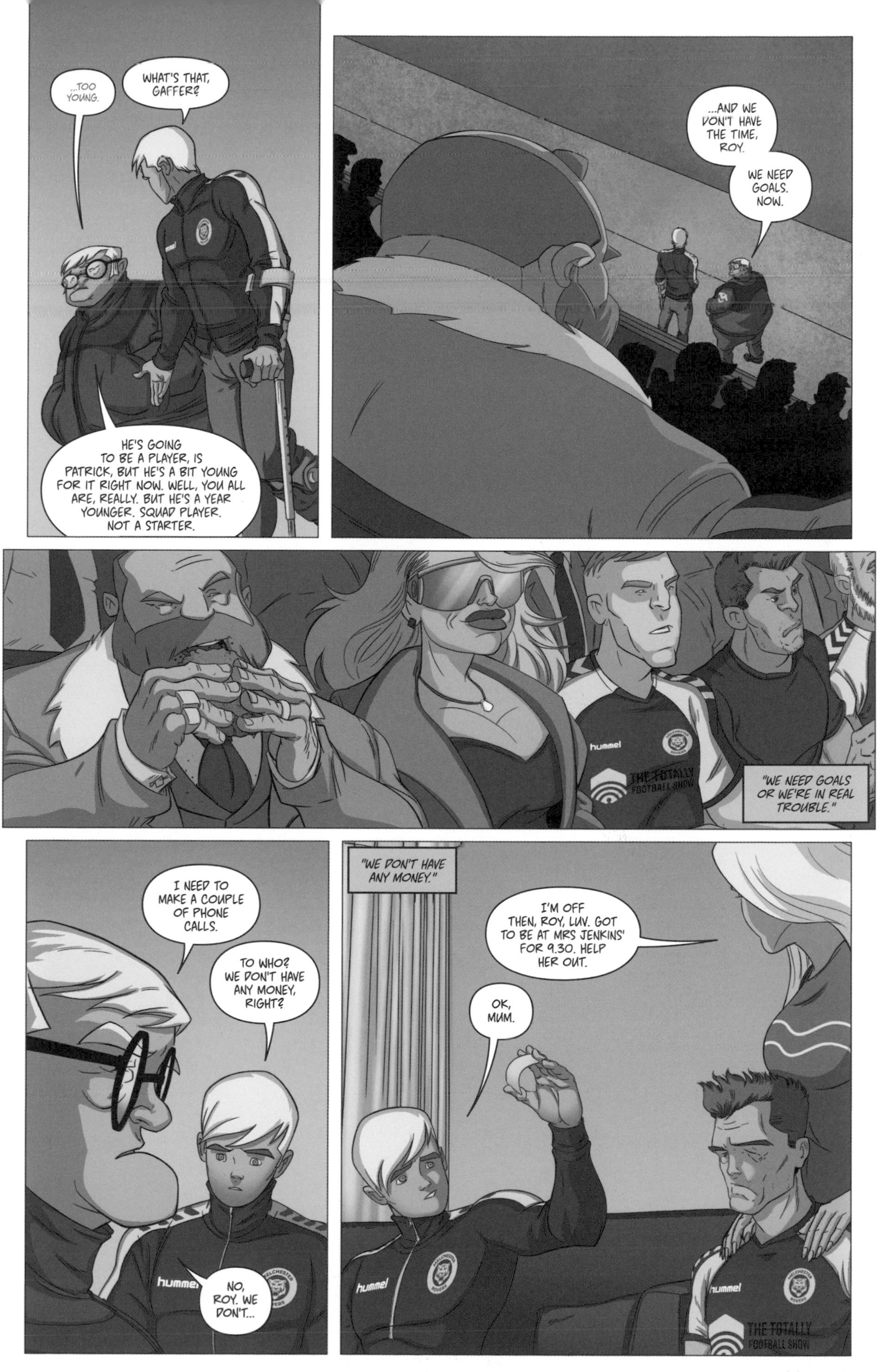
...TOO YOUNG.
WHAT'S THAT, GAFFER?
HE'S GOING TO BE A PLAYER, IS PATRICK, BUT HE'S A BIT YOUNG FOR IT RIGHT NOW. WELL, YOU ALL ARE, REALLY. BUT HE'S A YEAR YOUNGER. SQUAD PLAYER. NOT A STARTER.
...AND WE DON'T HAVE THE TIME, ROY.
WE NEED GOALS. NOW.
hummel
THE TOTALLY FOOTBALL SHOW
"WE NEED GOALS OR WE'RE IN REAL TROUBLE."
I NEED TO MAKE A COUPLE OF PHONE CALLS.
TO WHO? WE DON'T HAVE ANY MONEY, RIGHT?
hummel
NO, ROY. WE DON'T...
"WE DON'T HAVE ANY MONEY."
I'M OFF THEN, ROY, LUV. GOT TO BE AT MRS JENKINS' FOR 9.30. HELP HER OUT.
OK, MUM.
hummel
hummel
THE TOTALLY FOOTBALL SHOW

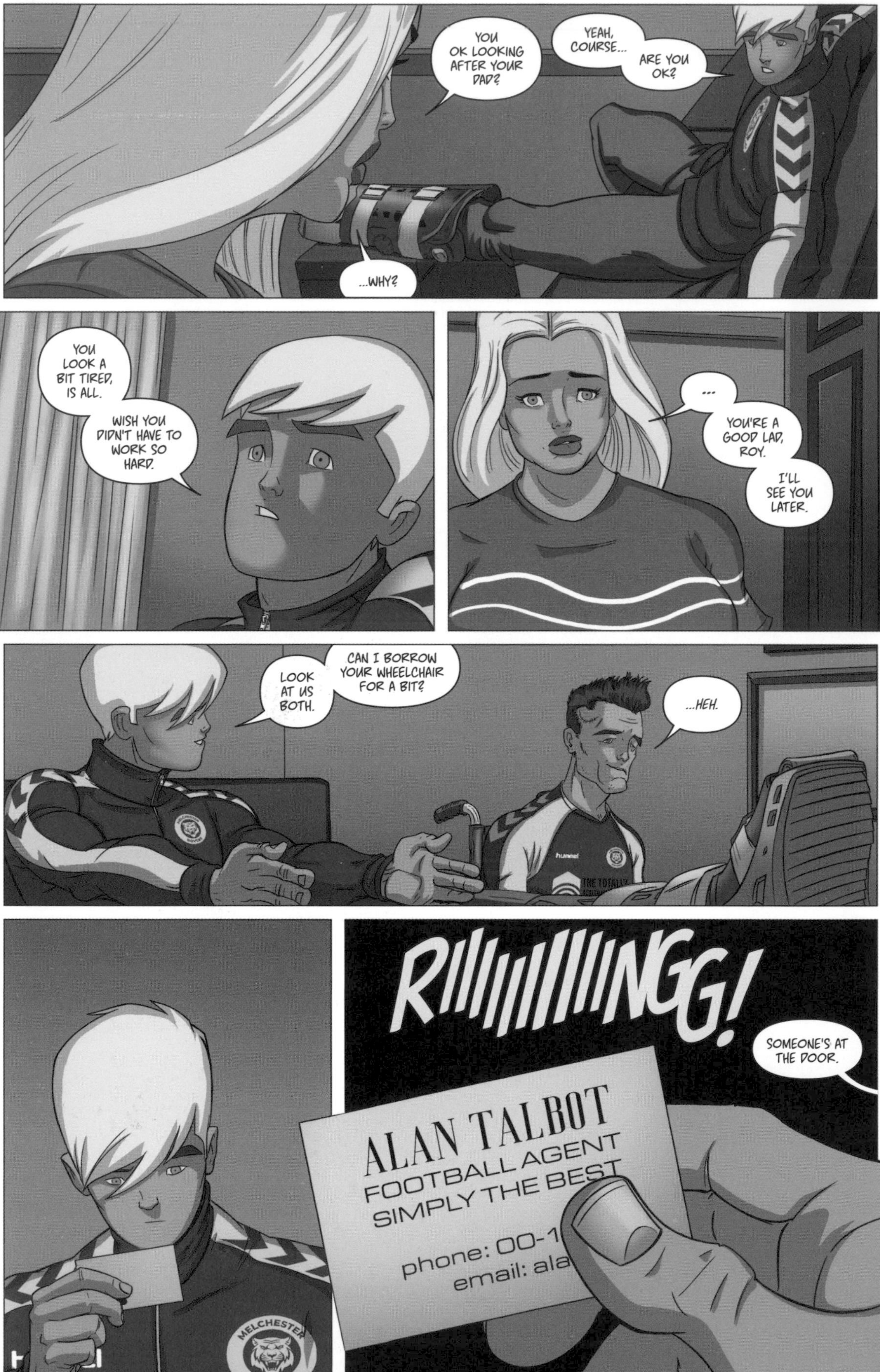
YOU OK LOOKING AFTER YOUR DAD?
YEAH, COURSE...
ARE YOU OK?
...WHY?
YOU LOOK A BIT TIRED, IS ALL.
WISH YOU DIDN'T HAVE TO WORK SO HARD.
...
YOU'RE A GOOD LAD, ROY.
I'LL SEE YOU LATER.
LOOK AT US BOTH.
CAN I BORROW YOUR WHEELCHAIR FOR A BIT?
...HEH.
hummel
MELCHESTER ROVERS
RIIIIIIIIIINGG!
SOMEONE'S AT THE DOOR.
ALAN TALBOT
FOOTBALL AGENT
SIMPLY THE BEST
phone: 00-1
email: ala

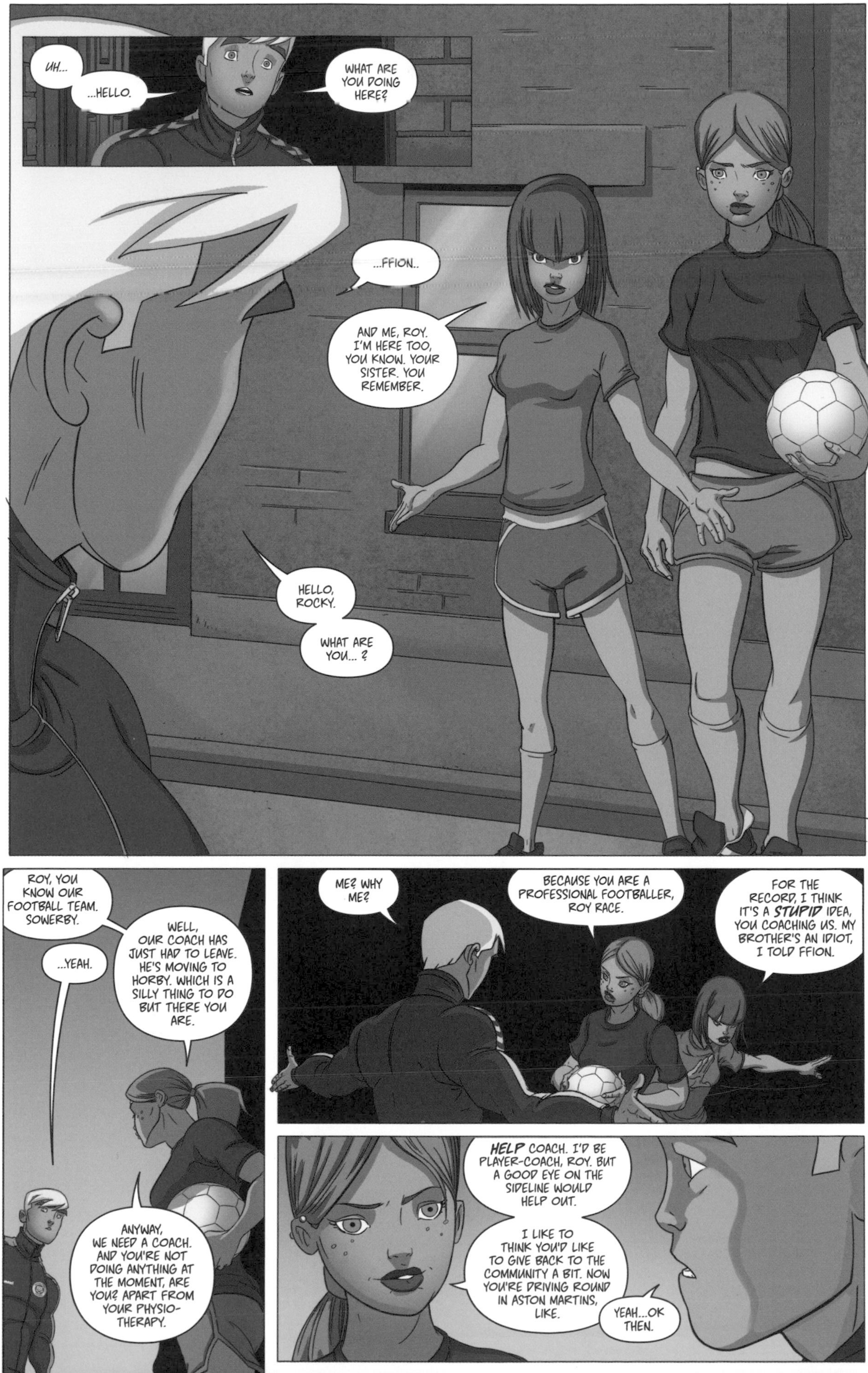
UH...
...HELLO.
WHAT ARE YOU DOING HERE?
...FFION..
AND ME, ROY. I'M HERE TOO, YOU KNOW. YOUR SISTER. YOU REMEMBER.
HELLO, ROCKY.
WHAT ARE YOU... ?
ROY, YOU KNOW OUR FOOTBALL TEAM. SOWERBY.
...YEAH.
WELL, OUR COACH HAS JUST HAD TO LEAVE. HE'S MOVING TO HORBY. WHICH IS A SILLY THING TO DO BUT THERE YOU ARE.
ANYWAY, WE NEED A COACH. AND YOU'RE NOT DOING ANYTHING AT THE MOMENT, ARE YOU? APART FROM YOUR PHYSIO-THERAPY.
ME? WHY ME?
BECAUSE YOU ARE A PROFESSIONAL FOOTBALLER, ROY RACE.
FOR THE RECORD, I THINK IT'S A STUPID IDEA, YOU COACHING US. MY BROTHER'S AN IDIOT, I TOLD FFION.
HELP COACH. I'D BE PLAYER-COACH, ROY. BUT A GOOD EYE ON THE SIDELINE WOULD HELP OUT.
I LIKE TO THINK YOU'D LIKE TO GIVE BACK TO THE COMMUNITY A BIT. NOW YOU'RE DRIVING ROUND IN ASTON MARTINS, LIKE.
YEAH...OK THEN.

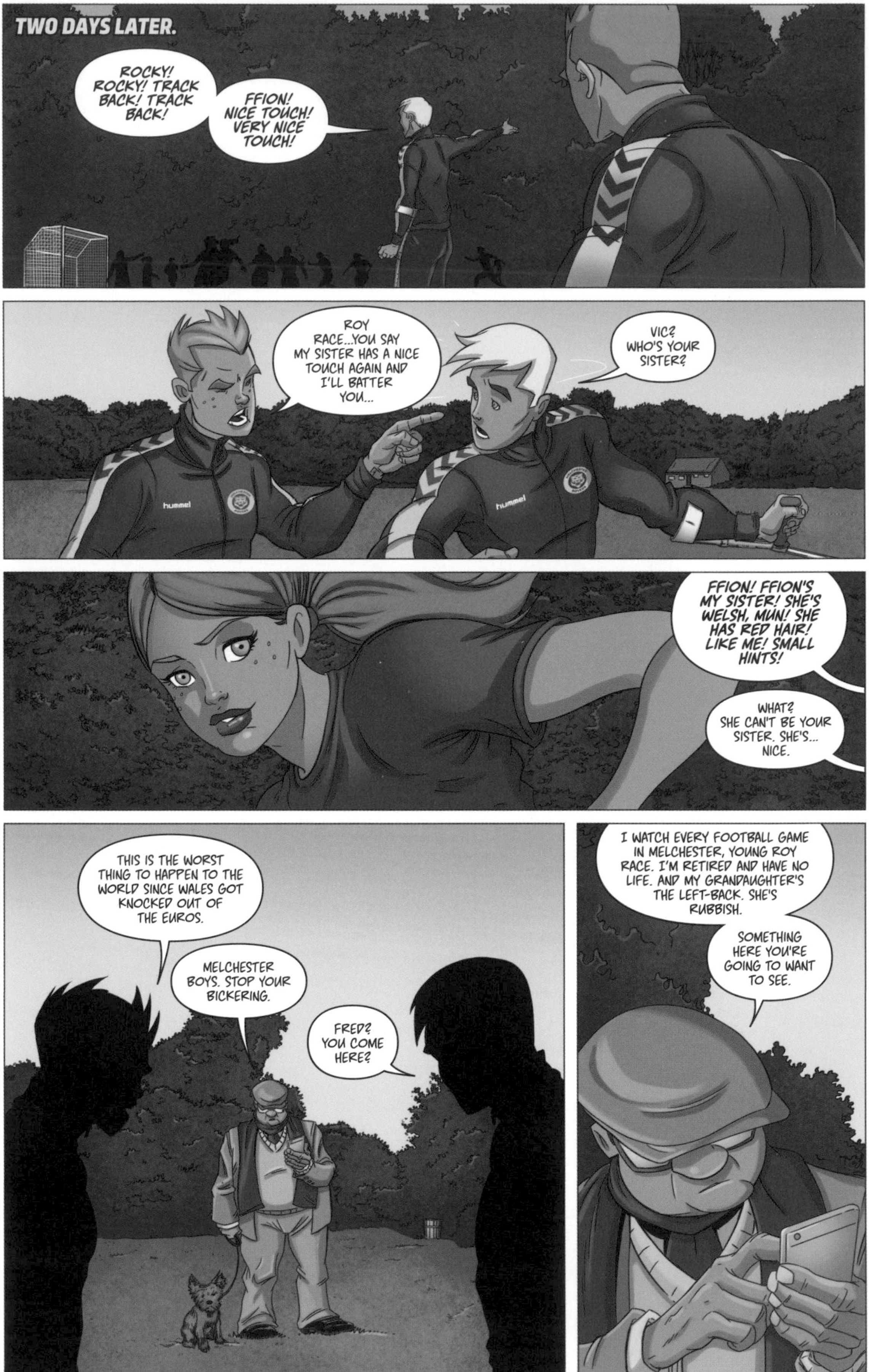
TWO DAYS LATER.
ROCKY! ROCKY! TRACK BACK! TRACK BACK!
FFION! NICE TOUCH! VERY NICE TOUCH!
ROY RACE...YOU SAY MY SISTER HAS A NICE TOUCH AGAIN AND I'LL BATTER YOU...
VIC? WHO'S YOUR SISTER?
FFION! FFION'S MY SISTER! SHE'S WELSH, MUN! SHE HAS RED HAIR! LIKE ME! SMALL HINTS!
WHAT? SHE CAN'T BE YOUR SISTER. SHE'S... NICE.
THIS IS THE WORST THING TO HAPPEN TO THE WORLD SINCE WALES GOT KNOCKED OUT OF THE EUROS.
MELCHESTER BOYS. STOP YOUR BICKERING.
FRED? YOU COME HERE?
I WATCH EVERY FOOTBALL GAME IN MELCHESTER, YOUNG ROY RACE. I'M RETIRED AND HAVE NO LIFE. AND MY GRANDAUGHTER'S THE LEFT-BACK. SHE'S RUBBISH.
SOMETHING HERE YOU'RE GOING TO WANT TO SEE.
hummel
hummel

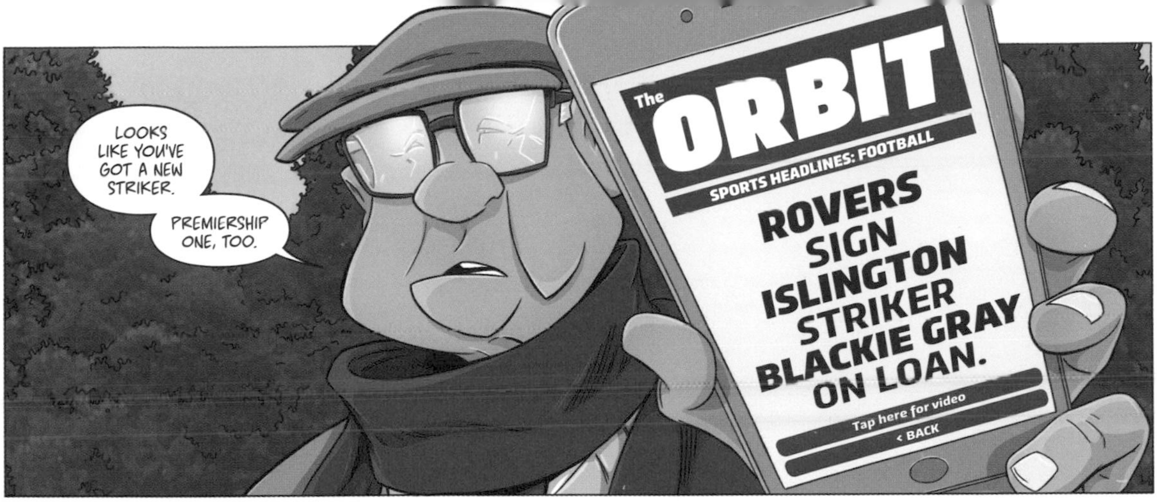
LOOKS LIKE YOU'VE GOT A NEW STRIKER.
PREMIERSHIP ONE, TOO.
The ORBIT
SPORTS HEADLINES: FOOTBALL
ROVERS SIGN ISLINGTON STRIKER BLACKIE GRAY ON LOAN.
Tap here for video
< BACK

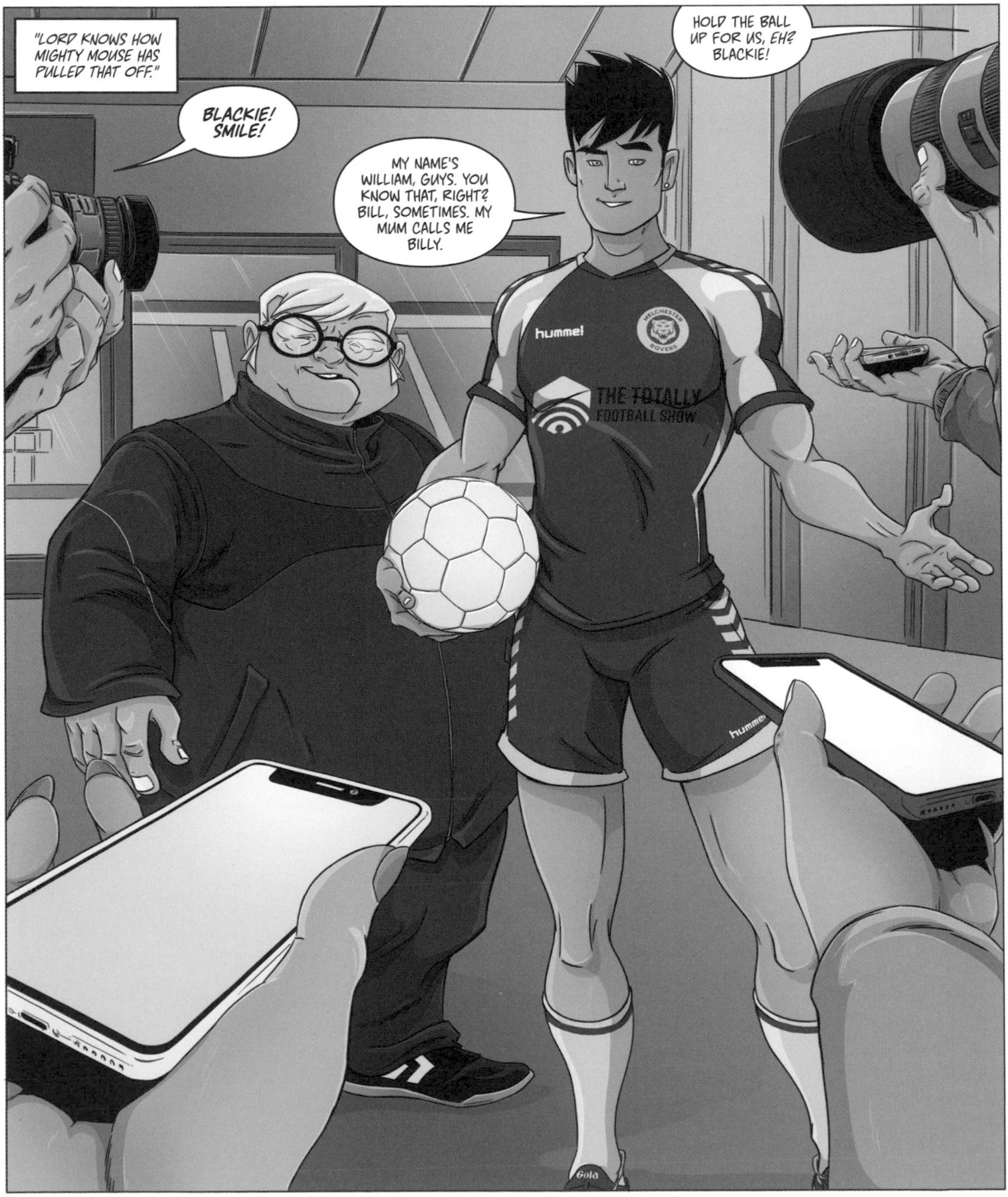
"LORD KNOWS HOW MIGHTY MOUSE HAS PULLED THAT OFF."
HOLD THE BALL UP FOR US, EH? BLACKIE!
BLACKIE! SMILE!
MY NAME'S WILLIAM, GUYS. YOU KNOW THAT, RIGHT? BILL, SOMETIMES. MY MUM CALLS ME BILLY.
hummel
MELCHESTER ROVERS
THE TOTALLY FOOTBALL SHOW

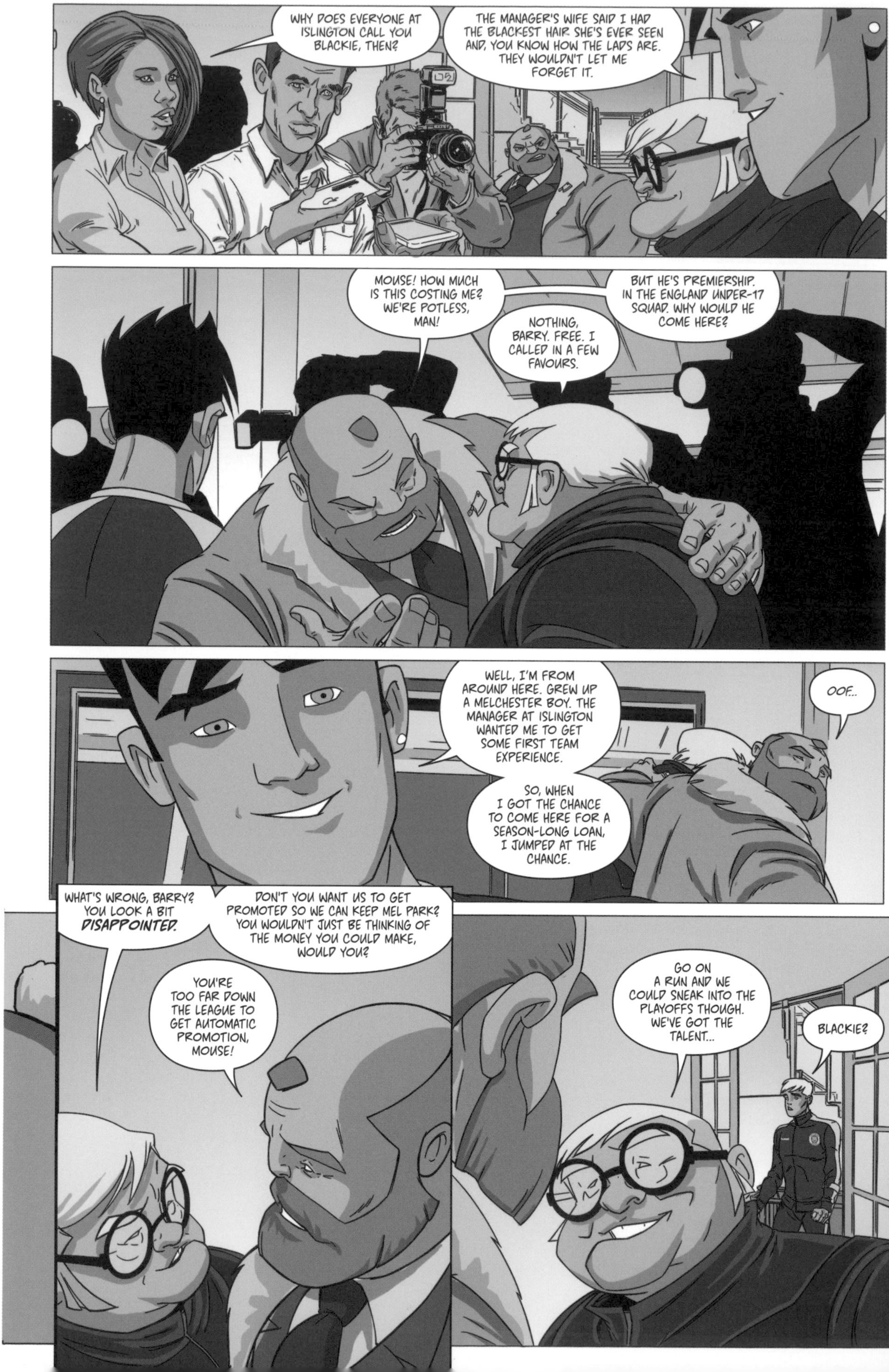
WHY DOES EVERYONE AT ISLINGTON CALL YOU BLACKIE, THEN?
THE MANAGER'S WIFE SAID I HAD THE BLACKEST HAIR SHE'S EVER SEEN AND, YOU KNOW HOW THE LADS ARE. THEY WOULDN'T LET ME FORGET IT.
MOUSE! HOW MUCH IS THIS COSTING ME? WE'RE POTLESS, MAN!
NOTHING, BARRY. FREE. I CALLED IN A FEW FAVOURS.
BUT HE'S PREMIERSHIP. IN THE ENGLAND UNDER-17 SQUAD. WHY WOULD HE COME HERE?
WELL, I'M FROM AROUND HERE. GREW UP A MELCHESTER BOY. THE MANAGER AT ISLINGTON WANTED ME TO GET SOME FIRST TEAM EXPERIENCE.
SO, WHEN I GOT THE CHANCE TO COME HERE FOR A SEASON-LONG LOAN, I JUMPED AT THE CHANCE.
OOF...
WHAT'S WRONG, BARRY? YOU LOOK A BIT ***DISAPPOINTED.***
DON'T YOU WANT US TO GET PROMOTED SO WE CAN KEEP MEL PARK? YOU WOULDN'T JUST BE THINKING OF THE MONEY YOU COULD MAKE, WOULD YOU?
YOU'RE TOO FAR DOWN THE LEAGUE TO GET AUTOMATIC PROMOTION, MOUSE!
GO ON A RUN AND WE COULD SNEAK INTO THE PLAYOFFS THOUGH. WE'VE GOT THE TALENT...
BLACKIE?

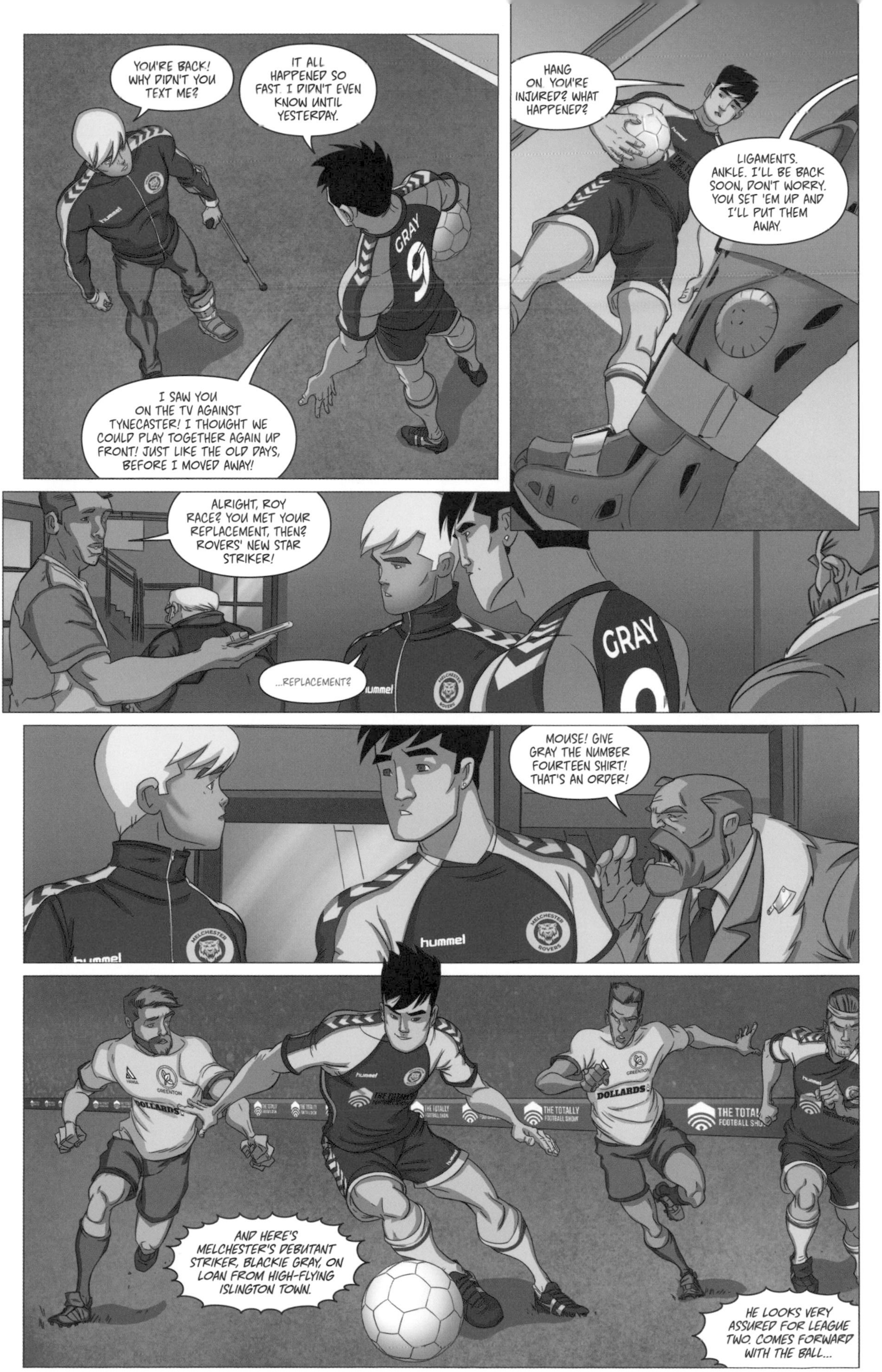

YOU'RE BACK! WHY DIDN'T YOU TEXT ME?
IT ALL HAPPENED SO FAST. I DIDN'T EVEN KNOW UNTIL YESTERDAY.
I SAW YOU ON THE TV AGAINST TYNECASTER! I THOUGHT WE COULD PLAY TOGETHER AGAIN UP FRONT! JUST LIKE THE OLD DAYS, BEFORE I MOVED AWAY!
GRAY
9
HANG ON. YOU'RE INJURED? WHAT HAPPENED?
LIGAMENTS. ANKLE. I'LL BE BACK SOON, DON'T WORRY. YOU SET 'EM UP AND I'LL PUT THEM AWAY.
ALRIGHT, ROY RACE? YOU MET YOUR REPLACEMENT, THEN? ROVERS' NEW STAR STRIKER!
...REPLACEMENT?
GRAY
MOUSE! GIVE GRAY THE NUMBER FOURTEEN SHIRT! THAT'S AN ORDER!
AND HERE'S MELCHESTER'S DEBUTANT STRIKER, BLACKIE GRAY, ON LOAN FROM HIGH-FLYING ISLINGTON TOWN.
HE LOOKS VERY ASSURED FOR LEAGUE TWO. COMES FORWARD WITH THE BALL...

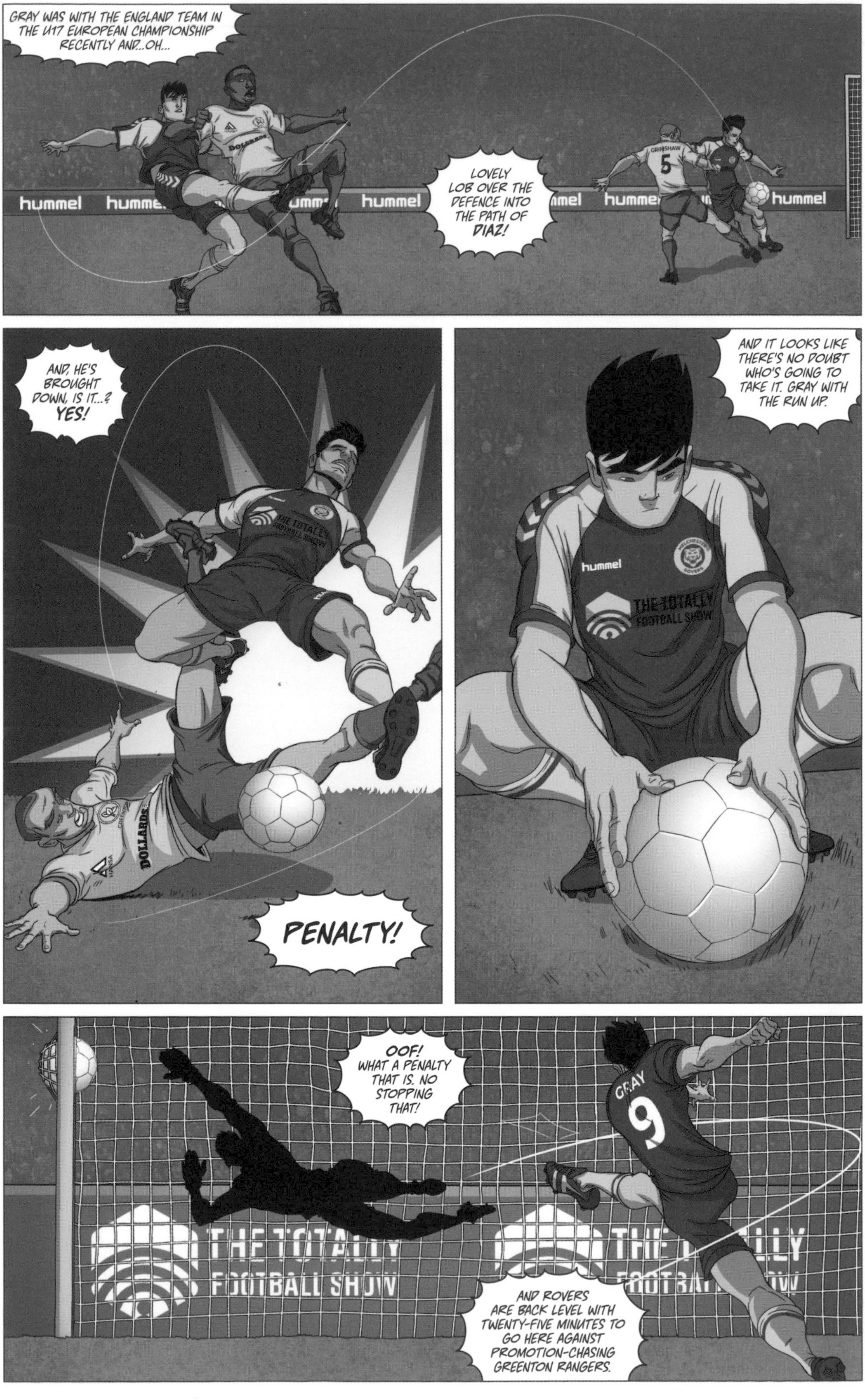
GRAY WAS WITH THE ENGLAND TEAM IN THE U17 EUROPEAN CHAMPIONSHIP RECENTLY AND...OH...
LOVELY LOB OVER THE DEFENCE INTO THE PATH OF DIAZ!
AND, HE'S BROUGHT DOWN, IS IT...? YES!
PENALTY!
AND IT LOOKS LIKE THERE'S NO DOUBT WHO'S GOING TO TAKE IT. GRAY WITH THE RUN UP.
OOF! WHAT A PENALTY THAT IS. NO STOPPING THAT!
AND ROVERS ARE BACK LEVEL WITH TWENTY-FIVE MINUTES TO GO HERE AGAINST PROMOTION-CHASING GREENTON RANGERS.

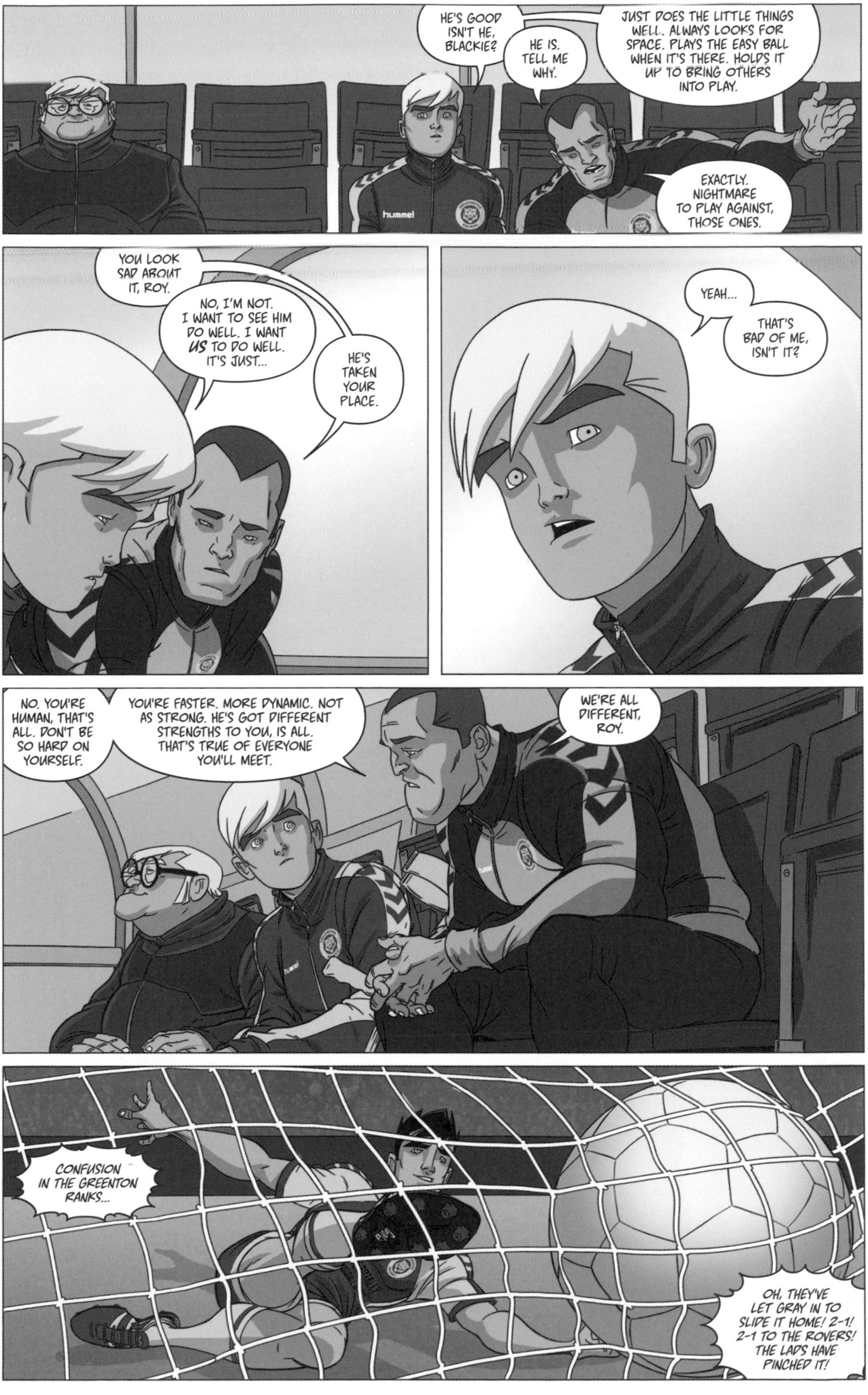
HE'S GOOD ISN'T HE, BLACKIE?
HE IS. TELL ME WHY.
JUST DOES THE LITTLE THINGS WELL. ALWAYS LOOKS FOR SPACE. PLAYS THE EASY BALL WHEN IT'S THERE. HOLDS IT UP TO BRING OTHERS INTO PLAY.
EXACTLY. NIGHTMARE TO PLAY AGAINST, THOSE ONES.
YOU LOOK SAD ABOUT IT, ROY.
NO, I'M NOT. I WANT TO SEE HIM DO WELL. I WANT US TO DO WELL. IT'S JUST...
HE'S TAKEN YOUR PLACE.
YEAH...
THAT'S BAD OF ME, ISN'T IT?
NO. YOU'RE HUMAN, THAT'S ALL. DON'T BE SO HARD ON YOURSELF.
YOU'RE FASTER. MORE DYNAMIC. NOT AS STRONG. HE'S GOT DIFFERENT STRENGTHS TO YOU, IS ALL. THAT'S TRUE OF EVERYONE YOU'LL MEET.
WE'RE ALL DIFFERENT, ROY.
CONFUSION IN THE GREENTON RANKS...
OH, THEY'VE LET GRAY IN TO SLIDE IT HOME! 2-1! 2-1 TO THE ROVERS! THE LADS HAVE PINCHED IT!

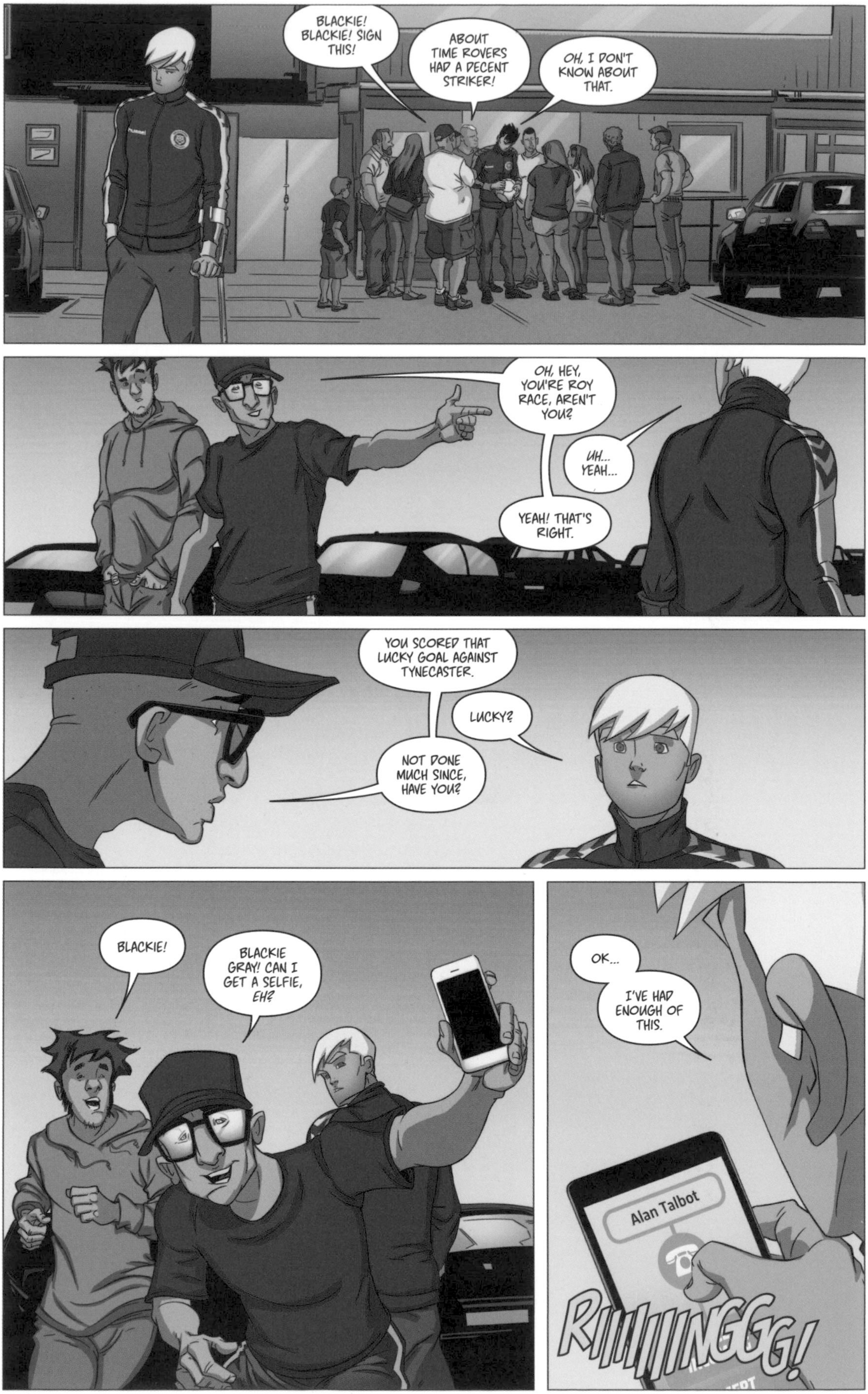
BLACKIE! BLACKIE! SIGN THIS!
ABOUT TIME ROVERS HAD A DECENT STRIKER!
OH, I DON'T KNOW ABOUT THAT.
OH, HEY, YOU'RE ROY RACE, AREN'T YOU?
UH... YEAH...
YEAH! THAT'S RIGHT.
YOU SCORED THAT LUCKY GOAL AGAINST TYNECASTER.
LUCKY?
NOT DONE MUCH SINCE, HAVE YOU?
BLACKIE!
BLACKIE GRAY! CAN I GET A SELFIE, EH?
OK...
I'VE HAD ENOUGH OF THIS.
Alan Talbot
RIIIIIINGGG!

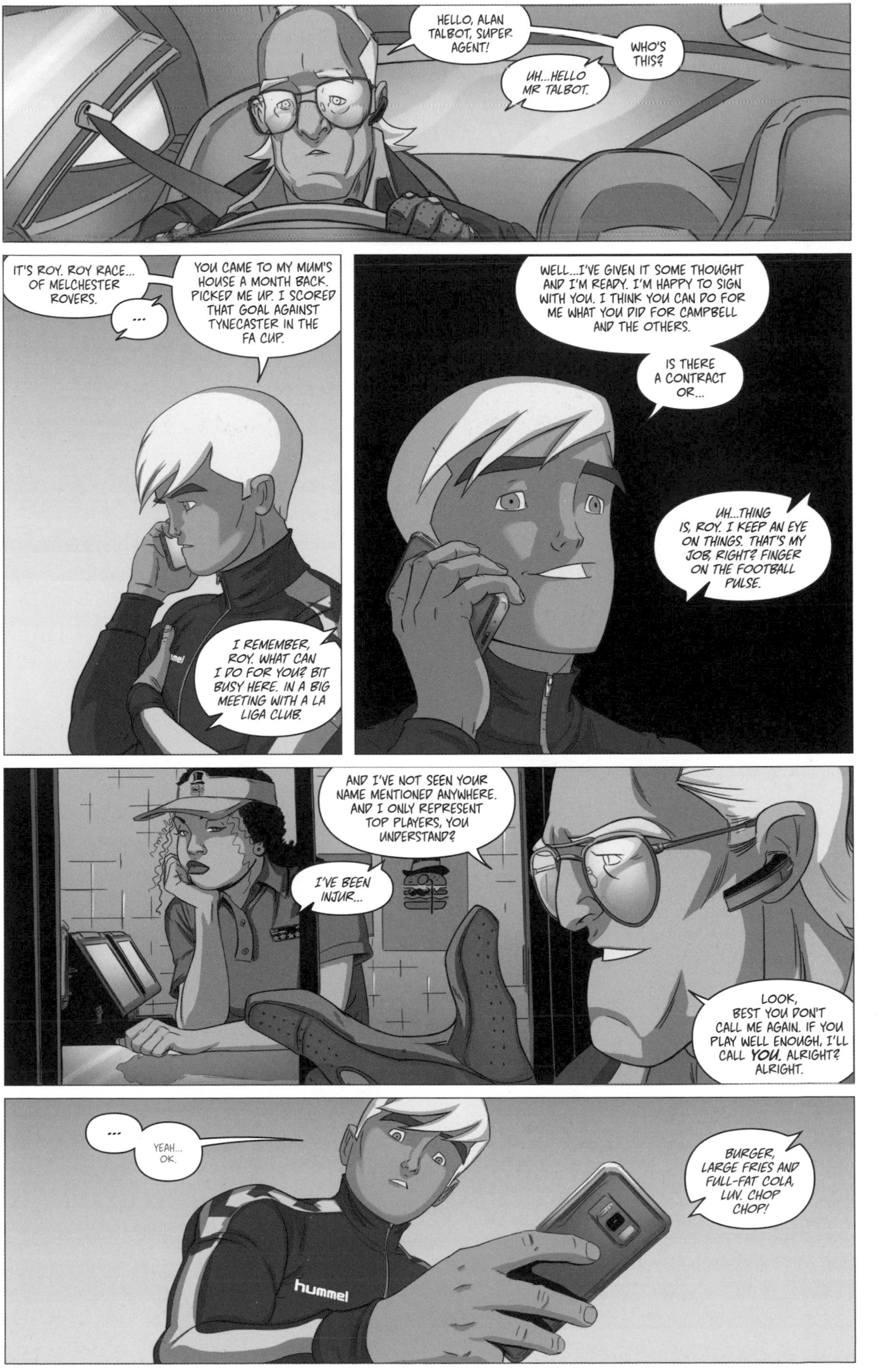
HELLO, ALAN TALBOT, SUPER AGENT!
WHO'S THIS?
UH...HELLO MR TALBOT.
IT'S ROY. ROY RACE... OF MELCHESTER ROVERS.
...
YOU CAME TO MY MUM'S HOUSE A MONTH BACK. PICKED ME UP. I SCORED THAT GOAL AGAINST TYNECASTER IN THE FA CUP.
I REMEMBER, ROY. WHAT CAN I DO FOR YOU? BIT BUSY HERE. IN A BIG MEETING WITH A LA LIGA CLUB.
WELL...I'VE GIVEN IT SOME THOUGHT AND I'M READY. I'M HAPPY TO SIGN WITH YOU. I THINK YOU CAN DO FOR ME WHAT YOU DID FOR CAMPBELL AND THE OTHERS.
IS THERE A CONTRACT OR...
UH...THING IS, ROY. I KEEP AN EYE ON THINGS. THAT'S MY JOB, RIGHT? FINGER ON THE FOOTBALL PULSE.
AND I'VE NOT SEEN YOUR NAME MENTIONED ANYWHERE. AND I ONLY REPRESENT TOP PLAYERS, YOU UNDERSTAND?
I'VE BEEN INJUR...
LOOK, BEST YOU DON'T CALL ME AGAIN. IF YOU PLAY WELL ENOUGH, I'LL CALL **YOU.** ALRIGHT? ALRIGHT.
...
YEAH... OK.
BURGER, LARGE FRIES AND FULL-FAT COLA, LUV. CHOP CHOP!

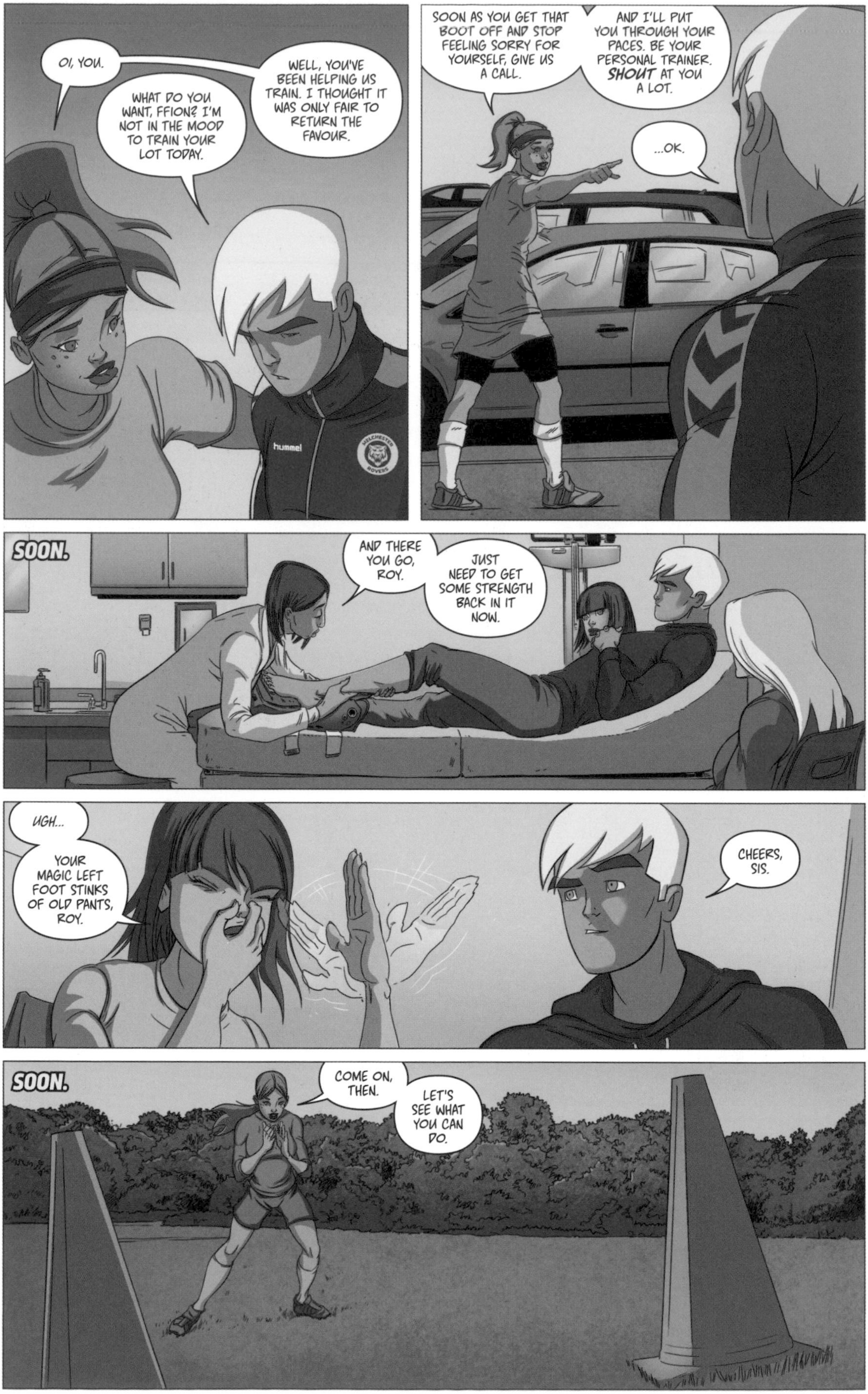
OI, YOU.
WHAT DO YOU WANT, FFION? I'M NOT IN THE MOOD TO TRAIN YOUR LOT TODAY.
WELL, YOU'VE BEEN HELPING US TRAIN. I THOUGHT IT WAS ONLY FAIR TO RETURN THE FAVOUR.
hummel
MELCHESTER ROVERS
SOON AS YOU GET THAT BOOT OFF AND STOP FEELING SORRY FOR YOURSELF, GIVE US A CALL.
AND I'LL PUT YOU THROUGH YOUR PACES. BE YOUR PERSONAL TRAINER. SHOUT AT YOU A LOT.
...OK.
SOON.
AND THERE YOU GO, ROY.
JUST NEED TO GET SOME STRENGTH BACK IN IT NOW.
UGH...
YOUR MAGIC LEFT FOOT STINKS OF OLD PANTS, ROY.
CHEERS, SIS.
SOON.
COME ON, THEN.
LET'S SEE WHAT YOU CAN DO.

STILL HURTS A BIT TO CHANGE DIRECTION.
DO IT OFTEN ENOUGH AND IT WON'T.
AND GRAY BEATS THE KEEPER AT THE NEAR POST! THAT'S 2-0 TO THE ROVERS!
TWO WINS ON THE BOUNCE FOR THE YOUNGSTERS OF MELCHESTER!
NNN...
I CAN SEE WHY MY BROTHER SHOUTS AT YOU. COME ON! FASTER! **DO IT!**
BLIMEY... WHAT IS... WRONG WITH YOUR...NNNN... FAMILY?
OUTRAGEOUS FROM DIAZ! THE SKILFUL SPANIARD PUTS THE ICING ON THE CAKE HERE IN ANOTHER WIN.
MELCHESTER ARE PUTTING AN EXCITING RUN TOGETHER HERE! THAT'S FOUR STRAIGHT WINS.
MID-TABLE NOW, BARRY. TEAMS ABOVE US KEEP DROPPING POINTS. GET THIRTEEN POINTS FROM OUR REMAINING FIVE GAMES AND WE MIGHT JUST SNEAK INTO THE PLAYOFFS.
BUT IT'S NOT AS THOUGH YOU **WANTED** TO SELL MEL PARK IS IT?
...COURSE NOT.

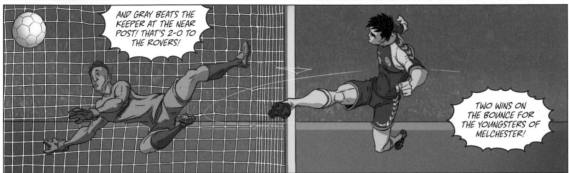

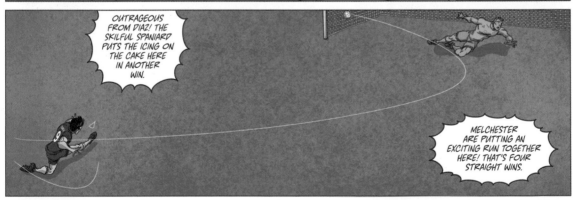

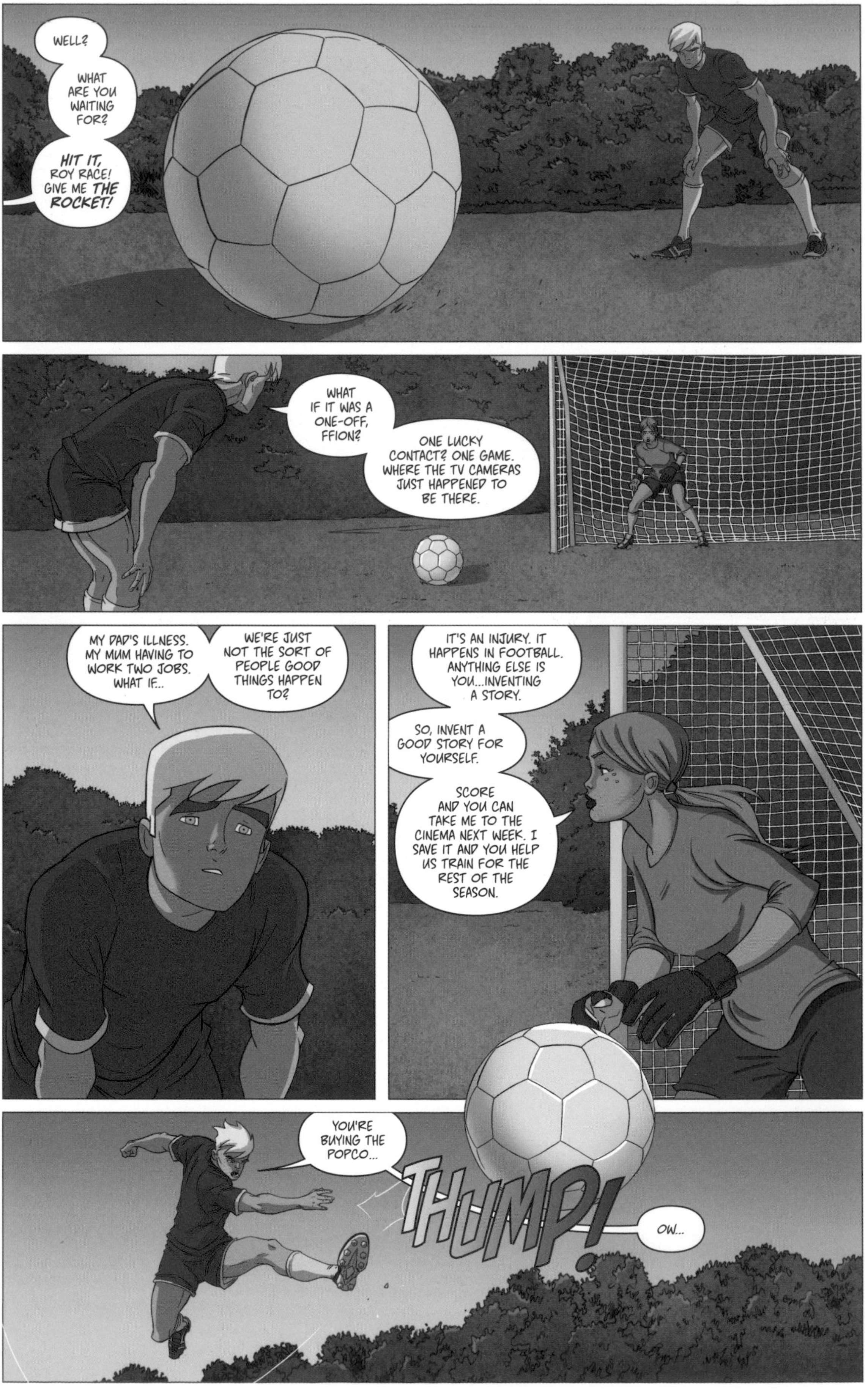
WELL?
WHAT ARE YOU WAITING FOR?
HIT IT, ROY RACE! GIVE ME **THE ROCKET!**
WHAT IF IT WAS A ONE-OFF, FFION?
ONE LUCKY CONTACT? ONE GAME. WHERE THE TV CAMERAS JUST HAPPENED TO BE THERE.
MY DAD'S ILLNESS. MY MUM HAVING TO WORK TWO JOBS. WHAT IF...
WE'RE JUST NOT THE SORT OF PEOPLE GOOD THINGS HAPPEN TO?
IT'S AN INJURY. IT HAPPENS IN FOOTBALL. ANYTHING ELSE IS YOU...INVENTING A STORY.
SO, INVENT A GOOD STORY FOR YOURSELF.
SCORE AND YOU CAN TAKE ME TO THE CINEMA NEXT WEEK. I SAVE IT AND YOU HELP US TRAIN FOR THE REST OF THE SEASON.
YOU'RE BUYING THE POPCO...
THUMP!
OW...

HA!

NICE TRY, RACE. ME AND THE GIRLS WILL SEE YOU EVERY MONDAY NIGHT FOR...

YOU OK?

I'M... I'M STILL NOT SURE IT'S RIGHT...

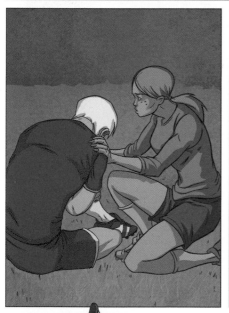

SOON.

ALRIGHT, FRED?

PREMIERSHIP SCOUT COMING TO THE GAME TONIGHT, ROY RACE. LOOKING AT PACO DIAZ. COUPLE OF CHAMPIONSHIP SCOUTS TOO.

HELP ROVERS WIN THEIR LAST THREE GAMES IF YOU WANT TO KEEP YOUR PAL AROUND.

HI, MUM, DAD.

JOHNNY DEXTER PHONED, LOVE. TWICE.

YEAH, MY PHONE'S OUT OF JUICE. WHAT'S THIS?

DUNNO. DELIVERY FROM EARLIER. CAME FOR YOU.

RIIIIIIPPP!

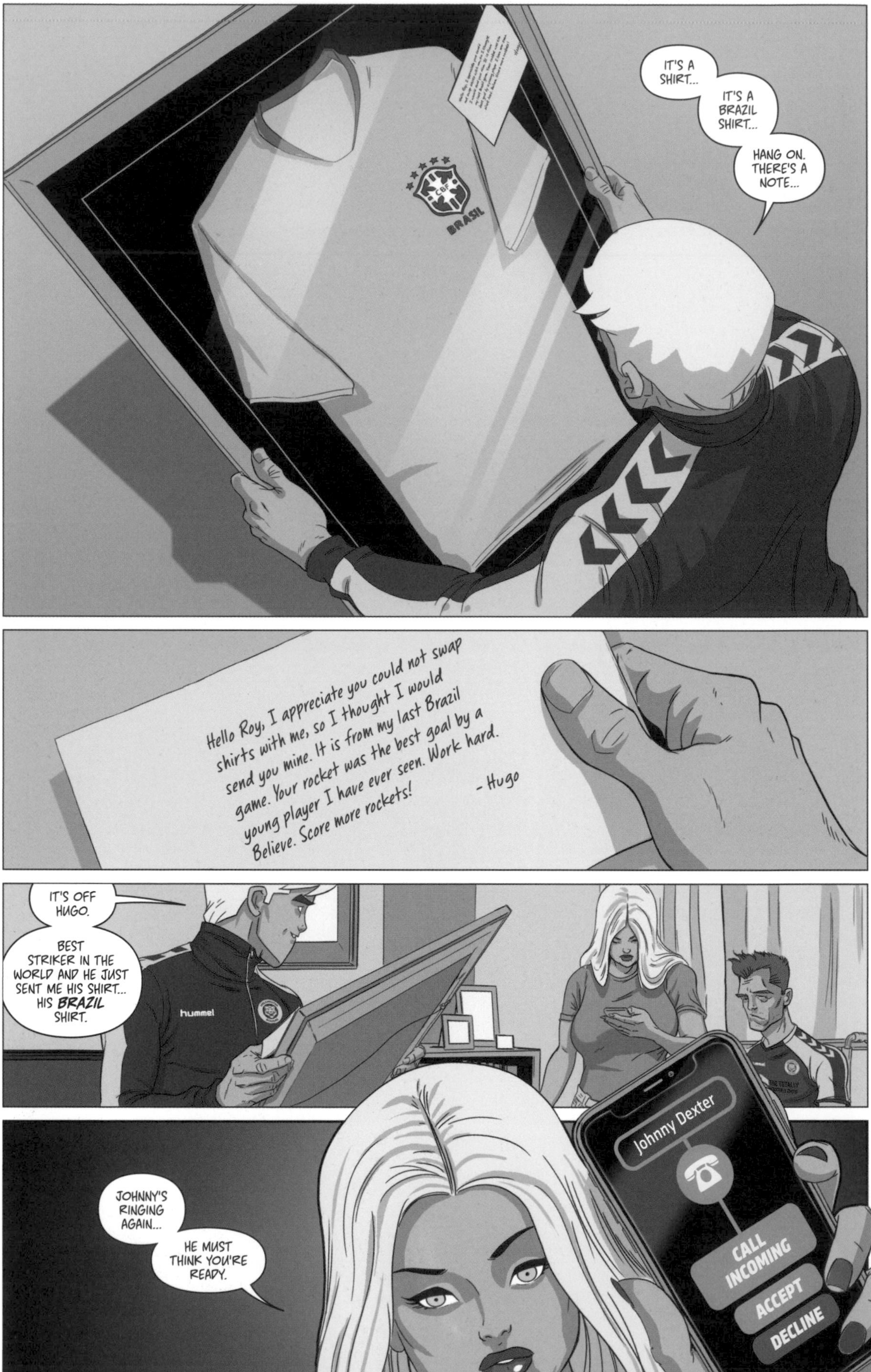
IT'S A SHIRT...
IT'S A BRAZIL SHIRT...
HANG ON. THERE'S A NOTE...
Hello Roy, I appreciate you could not swap shirts with me, so I thought I would send you mine. It is from my last Brazil game. Your rocket was the best goal by a young player I have ever seen. Work hard. Believe. Score more rockets!
- Hugo
IT'S OFF HUGO.
BEST STRIKER IN THE WORLD AND HE JUST SENT ME HIS SHIRT... HIS BRAZIL SHIRT.
JOHNNY'S RINGING AGAIN...
HE MUST THINK YOU'RE READY.
Johnny Dexter
CALL INCOMING
ACCEPT
DECLINE

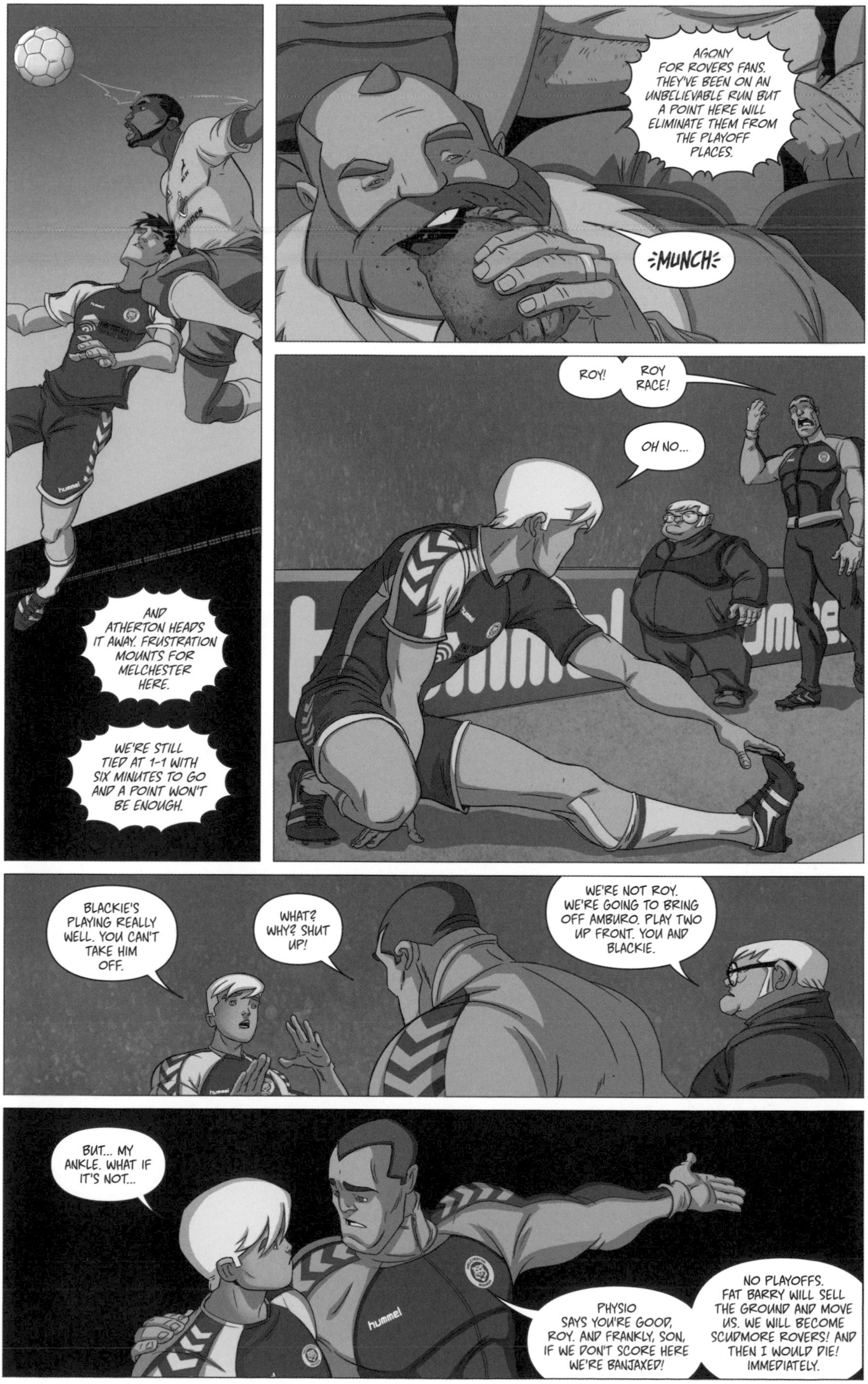
AND ATHERTON HEADS IT AWAY. FRUSTRATION MOUNTS FOR MELCHESTER HERE.
WE'RE STILL TIED AT 1-1 WITH SIX MINUTES TO GO AND A POINT WON'T BE ENOUGH.
AGONY FOR ROVERS FANS. THEY'VE BEEN ON AN UNBELIEVABLE RUN BUT A POINT HERE WILL ELIMINATE THEM FROM THE PLAYOFF PLACES.
MUNCH
ROY!
ROY RACE!
OH NO...
hummel
BLACKIE'S PLAYING REALLY WELL. YOU CAN'T TAKE HIM OFF.
WHAT? WHY? SHUT UP!
WE'RE NOT ROY. WE'RE GOING TO BRING OFF AMBURO. PLAY TWO UP FRONT. YOU AND BLACKIE.
BUT... MY ANKLE. WHAT IF IT'S NOT...
PHYSIO SAYS YOU'RE GOOD, ROY. AND FRANKLY, SON, IF WE DON'T SCORE HERE WE'RE BANJAXED!
NO PLAYOFFS. FAT BARRY WILL SELL THE GROUND AND MOVE US. WE WILL BECOME SCUDMORE ROVERS! AND THEN I WOULD DIE! IMMEDIATELY.
hummel

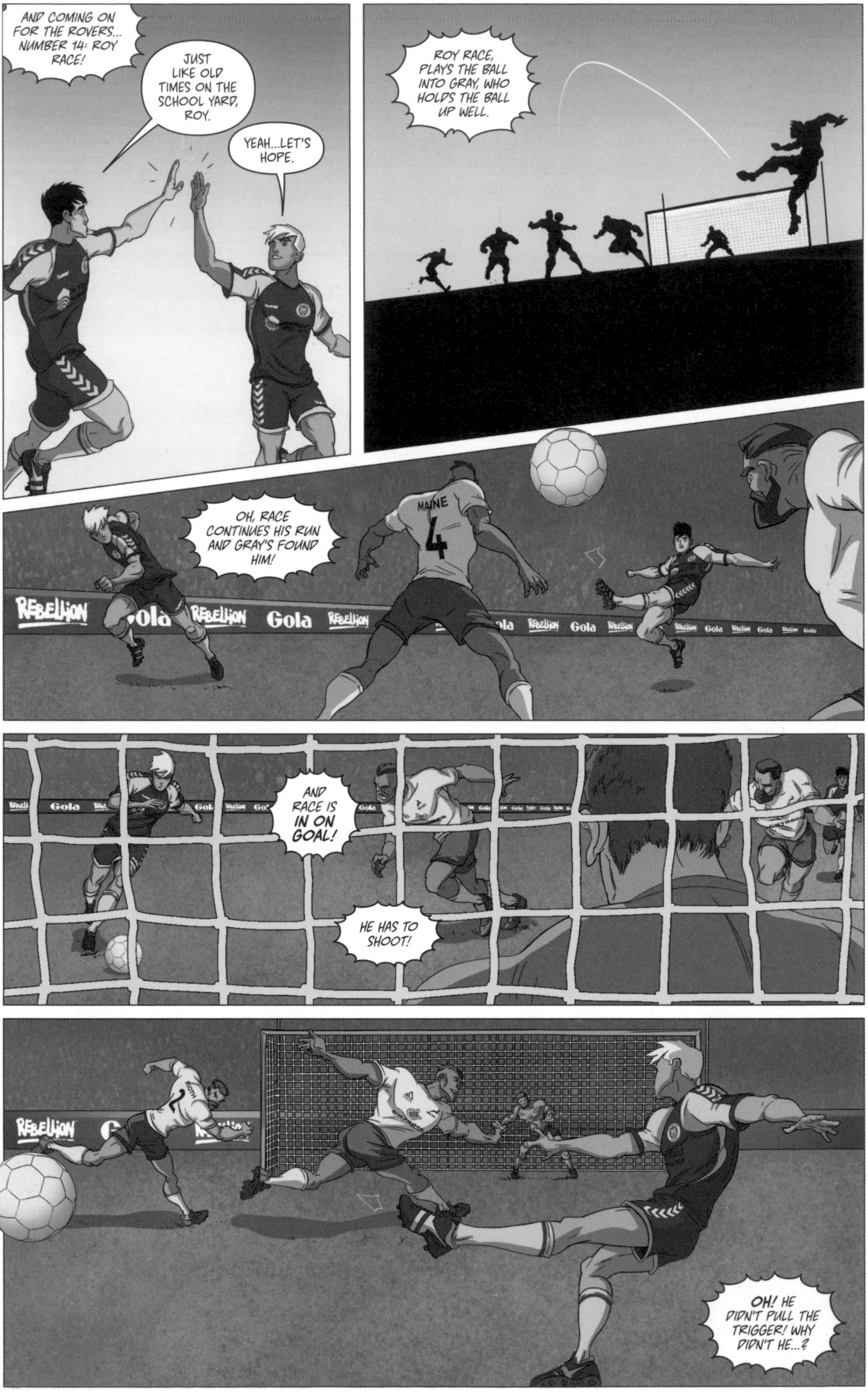
AND COMING ON FOR THE ROVERS... NUMBER 14: ROY RACE!
JUST LIKE OLD TIMES ON THE SCHOOL YARD, ROY.
YEAH...LET'S HOPE.
ROY RACE, PLAYS THE BALL INTO GRAY, WHO HOLDS THE BALL UP WELL.
MAINE
4
OH, RACE CONTINUES HIS RUN AND GRAY'S FOUND HIM!
REBELLION
Gola
AND RACE IS IN ON GOAL!
HE HAS TO SHOOT!
OH! HE DIDN'T PULL THE TRIGGER! WHY DIDN'T HE...?

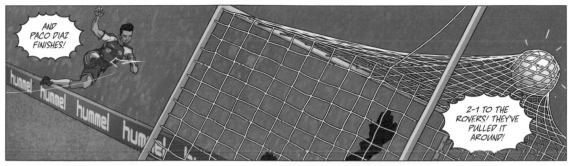

AND PACO DIAZ FINISHES!

2-1 TO THE ROVERS! THEY'VE PULLED IT AROUND!

AND IT'S EARLY DAYS BUT YOU HAVE TO LIKE THE LOOK OF THAT ROY RACE-BLACKIE GRAY PARTNERSHIP UP FRONT!

TERRIFIC MOVEMENT AND A GREAT UNDERSTANDING. THE TWO COMPLEMENT EACH OTHER SO WELL.

AND THERE'S THE FINAL WHISTLE! THREE POINTS!

AFTER THE START THEY HAD TO THE SEASON, AND THE YOUTH OF THIS MELCHESTER TEAM, THIS RUN IS AN AMAZING FEAT!

...BRILLIANT...

YOU SEE THAT, GAFFER! ROY'S MOVEMENT. THEY COULDN'T DEAL WITH IT.

YEAH, I SAW, BOYS. I SAW.

DIDN'T HIT IT THOUGH, DID YOU? AND YOU COULD HAVE.

TRUST THAT LEFT FOOT OF YOURS, EH?

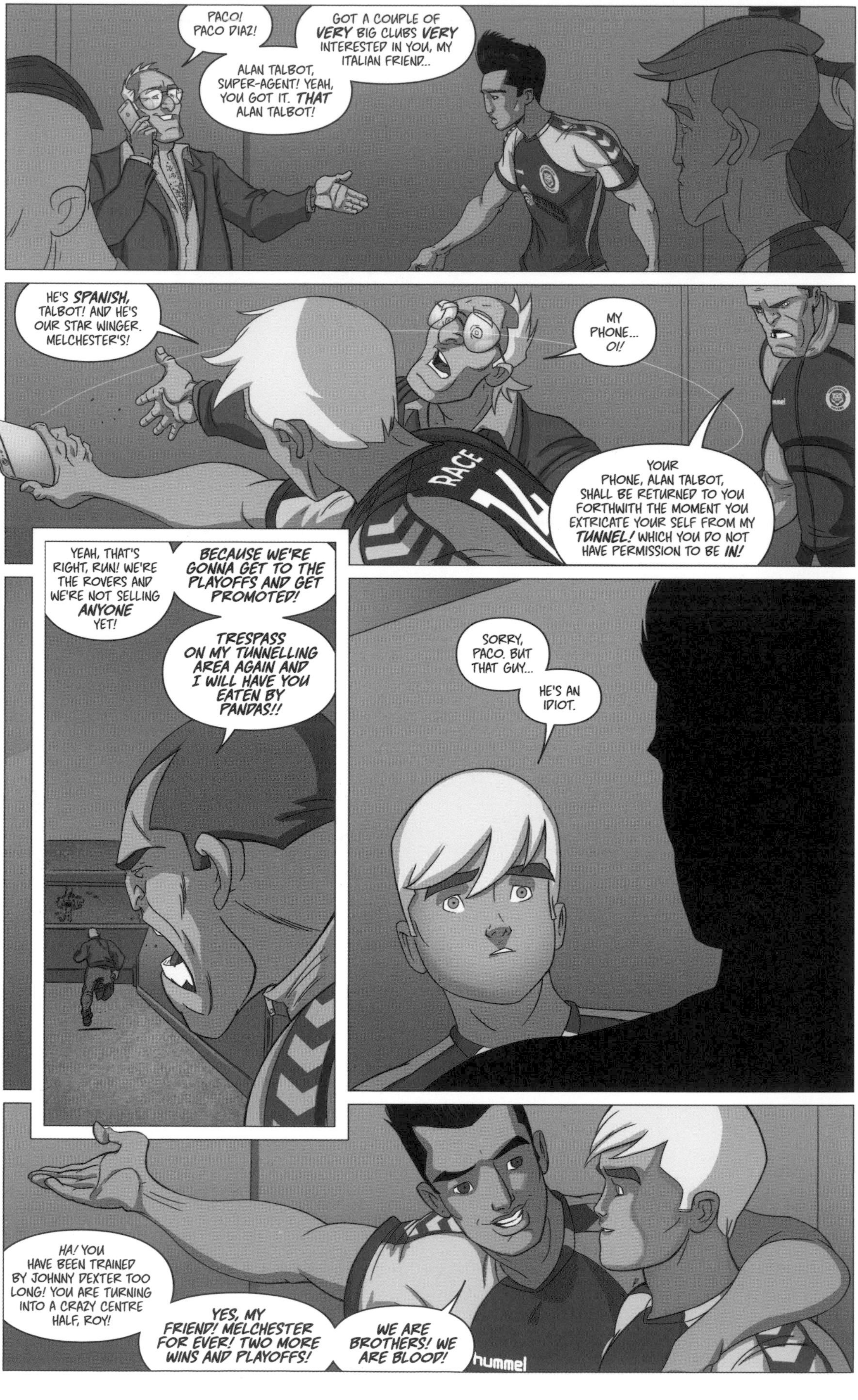
PACO! PACO DIAZ!
GOT A COUPLE OF VERY BIG CLUBS VERY INTERESTED IN YOU, MY ITALIAN FRIEND...
ALAN TALBOT, SUPER-AGENT! YEAH, YOU GOT IT. THAT ALAN TALBOT!
HE'S SPANISH, TALBOT! AND HE'S OUR STAR WINGER. MELCHESTER'S!
MY PHONE... OI!
RACE
YOUR PHONE, ALAN TALBOT, SHALL BE RETURNED TO YOU FORTHWITH THE MOMENT YOU EXTRICATE YOUR SELF FROM MY TUNNEL! WHICH YOU DO NOT HAVE PERMISSION TO BE IN!
YEAH, THAT'S RIGHT, RUN! WE'RE THE ROVERS AND WE'RE NOT SELLING ANYONE YET!
BECAUSE WE'RE GONNA GET TO THE PLAYOFFS AND GET PROMOTED!
TRESPASS ON MY TUNNELLING AREA AGAIN AND I WILL HAVE YOU EATEN BY PANDAS!!
SORRY, PACO. BUT THAT GUY...
HE'S AN IDIOT.
HA! YOU HAVE BEEN TRAINED BY JOHNNY DEXTER TOO LONG! YOU ARE TURNING INTO A CRAZY CENTRE HALF, ROY!
YES, MY FRIEND! MELCHESTER FOR EVER! TWO MORE WINS AND PLAYOFFS!
WE ARE BROTHERS! WE ARE BLOOD!
hummel

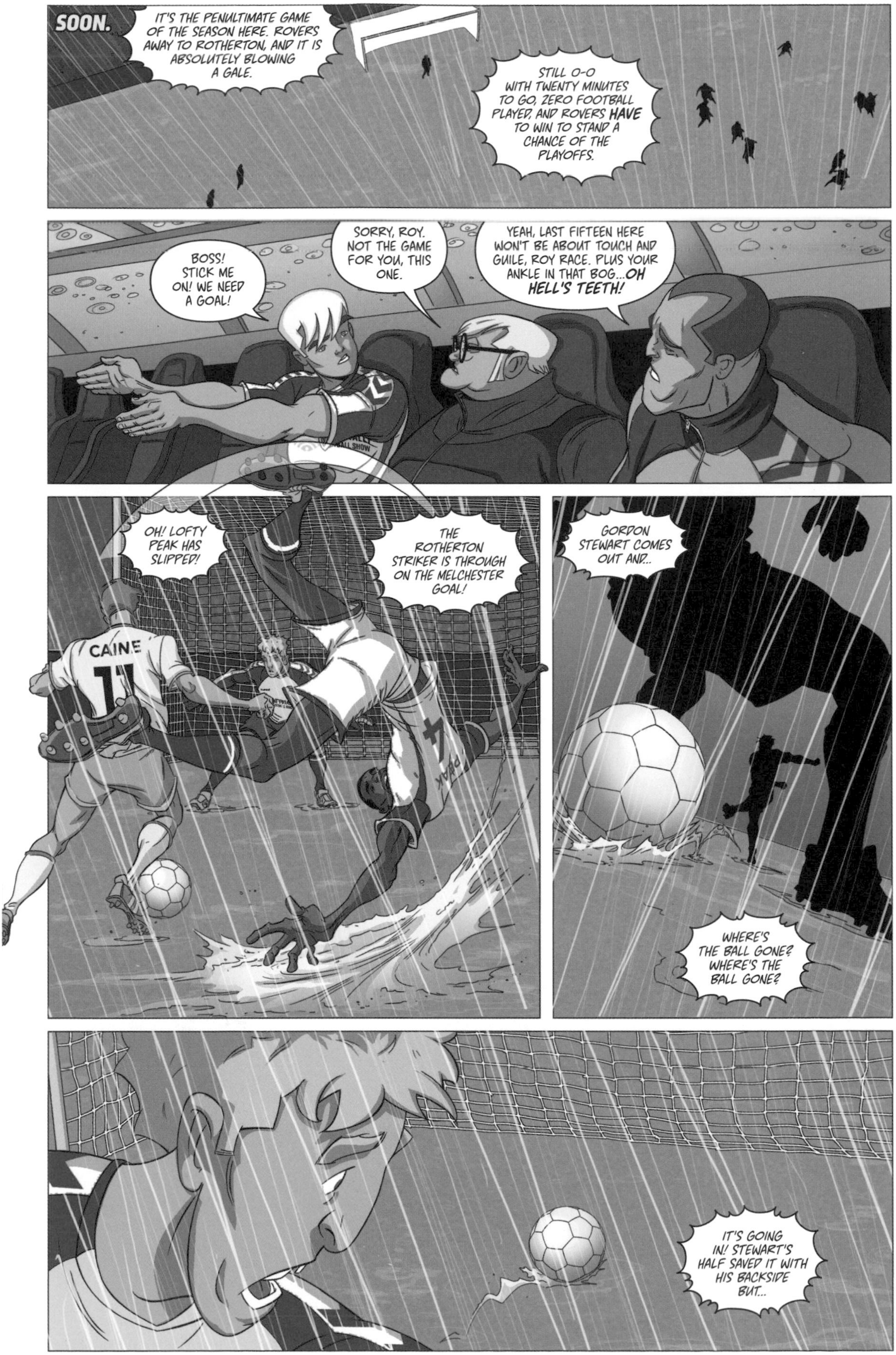
SOON.
IT'S THE PENULTIMATE GAME OF THE SEASON HERE. ROVERS AWAY TO ROTHERTON, AND IT IS ABSOLUTELY BLOWING A GALE.
STILL 0-0 WITH TWENTY MINUTES TO GO, ZERO FOOTBALL PLAYED, AND ROVERS HAVE TO WIN TO STAND A CHANCE OF THE PLAYOFFS.
BOSS! STICK ME ON! WE NEED A GOAL!
SORRY, ROY. NOT THE GAME FOR YOU, THIS ONE.
YEAH, LAST FIFTEEN HERE WON'T BE ABOUT TOUCH AND GUILE, ROY RACE. PLUS YOUR ANKLE IN THAT BOG...OH HELL'S TEETH!
OH! LOFTY PEAK HAS SLIPPED!
THE ROTHERTON STRIKER IS THROUGH ON THE MELCHESTER GOAL!
CAINE
11
PEAK
4
GORDON STEWART COMES OUT AND...
WHERE'S THE BALL GONE? WHERE'S THE BALL GONE?
IT'S GOING IN! STEWART'S HALF SAVED IT WITH HIS BACKSIDE BUT...

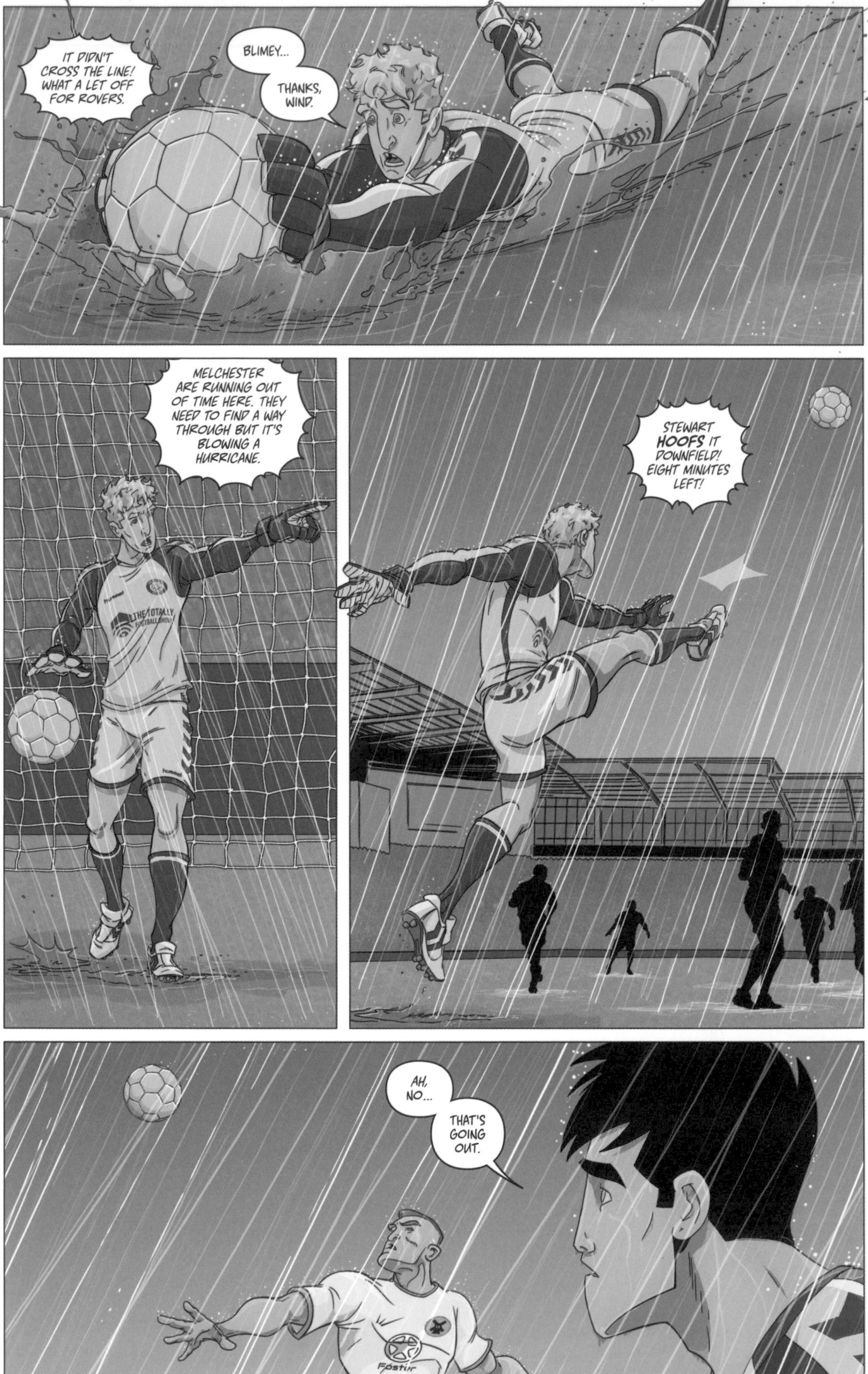

IT DIDN'T CROSS THE LINE! WHAT A LET OFF FOR ROVERS.
BLIMEY...
THANKS, WIND.
MELCHESTER ARE RUNNING OUT OF TIME HERE. THEY NEED TO FIND A WAY THROUGH BUT IT'S BLOWING A HURRICANE.
STEWART **HOOFS** IT DOWNFIELD! EIGHT MINUTES LEFT!
AH, NO...
THAT'S GOING OUT.

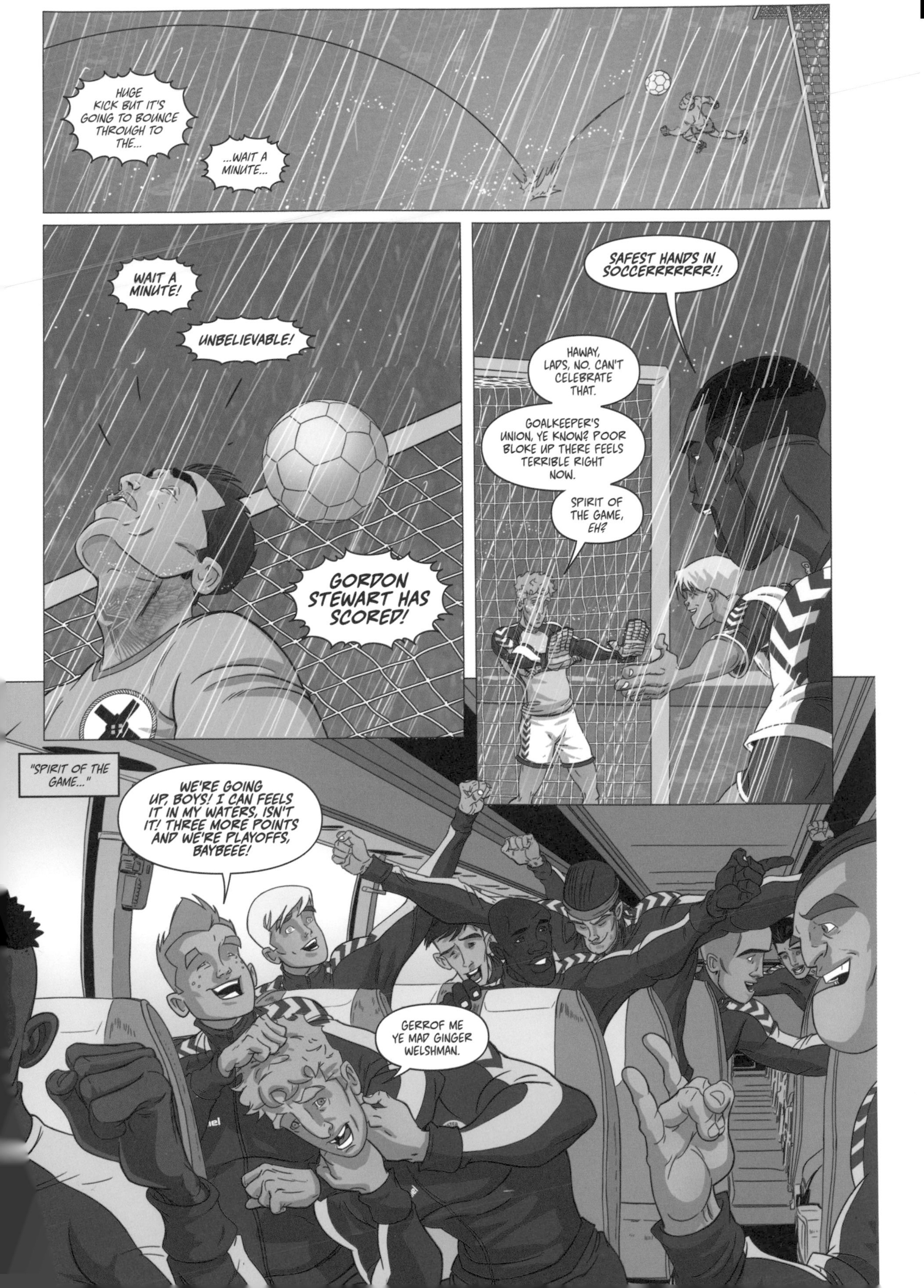
HUGE KICK BUT IT'S GOING TO BOUNCE THROUGH TO THE...
...WAIT A MINUTE...
WAIT A MINUTE!
UNBELIEVABLE!
GORDON STEWART HAS SCORED!
SAFEST HANDS IN SOCCERRRRRRR!!
HAWAY, LADS, NO. CAN'T CELEBRATE THAT.
GOALKEEPER'S UNION, YE KNOW? POOR BLOKE UP THERE FEELS TERRIBLE RIGHT NOW.
SPIRIT OF THE GAME, EH?
"SPIRIT OF THE GAME..."
WE'RE GOING UP, BOYS! I CAN FEELS IT IN MY WATERS, ISN'T IT! THREE MORE POINTS AND WE'RE PLAYOFFS, BAYBEEE!
GERROF ME YE MAD GINGER WELSHMAN.

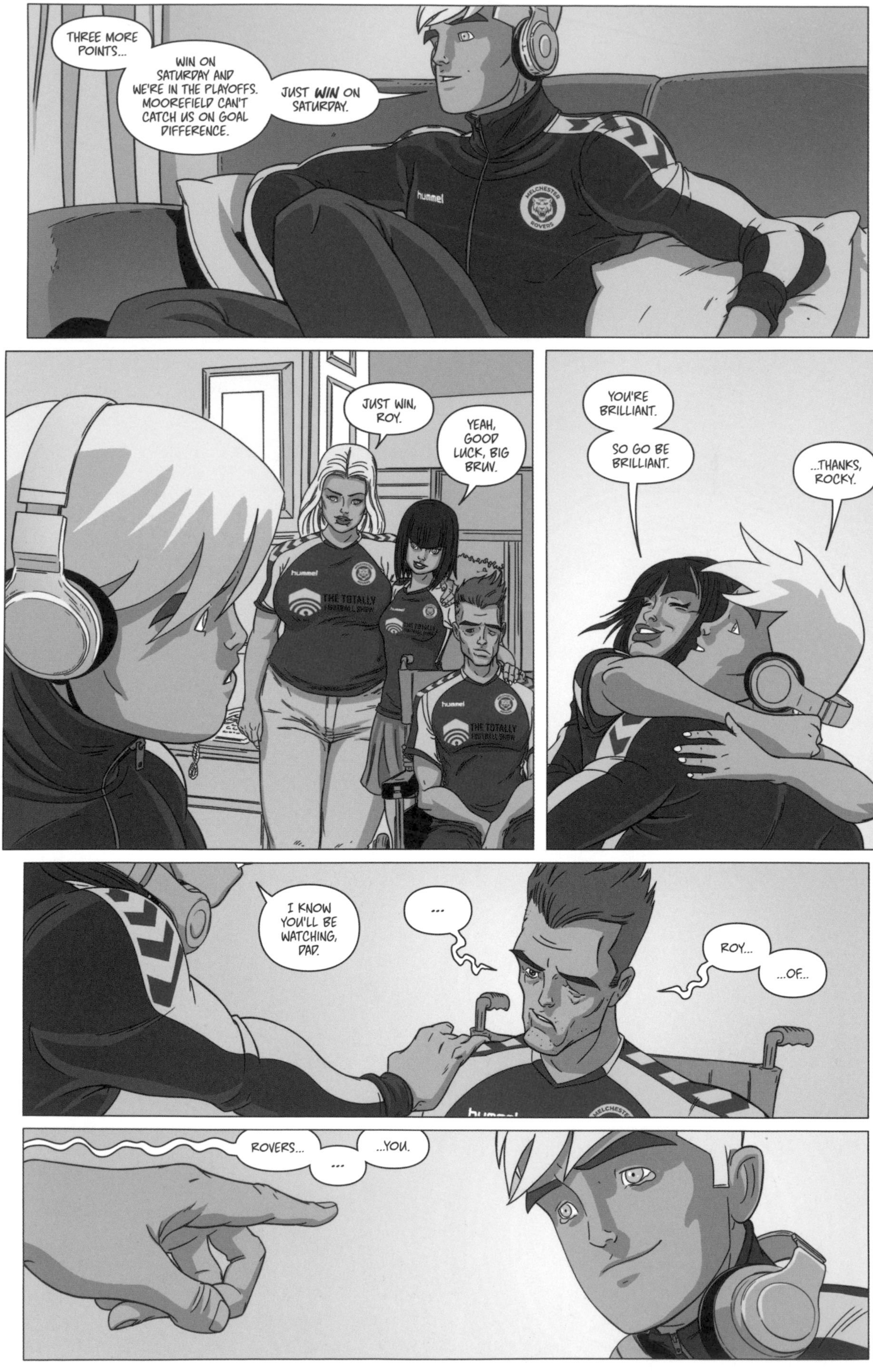
THREE MORE POINTS...
WIN ON SATURDAY AND WE'RE IN THE PLAYOFFS. MOOREFIELD CAN'T CATCH US ON GOAL DIFFERENCE.
JUST WIN ON SATURDAY.
JUST WIN, ROY.
YEAH, GOOD LUCK, BIG BRUV.
YOU'RE BRILLIANT.
SO GO BE BRILLIANT.
...THANKS, ROCKY.
I KNOW YOU'LL BE WATCHING, DAD.
...
ROY...
...OF...
ROVERS...
...
...YOU.

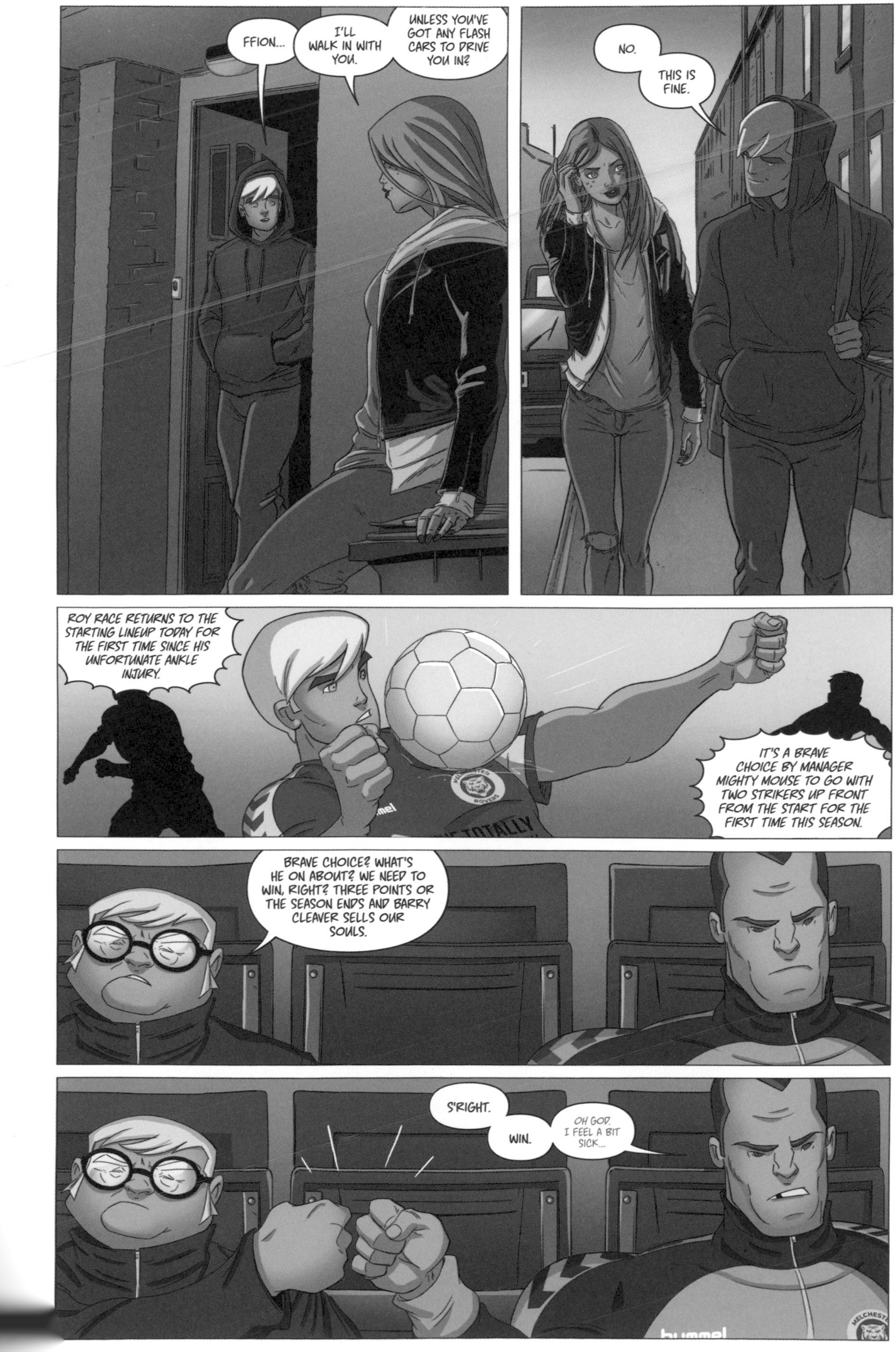
FFION...
I'LL WALK IN WITH YOU.
UNLESS YOU'VE GOT ANY FLASH CARS TO DRIVE YOU IN?
NO.
THIS IS FINE.
ROY RACE RETURNS TO THE STARTING LINEUP TODAY FOR THE FIRST TIME SINCE HIS UNFORTUNATE ANKLE INJURY.
IT'S A BRAVE CHOICE BY MANAGER MIGHTY MOUSE TO GO WITH TWO STRIKERS UP FRONT FROM THE START FOR THE FIRST TIME THIS SEASON.
BRAVE CHOICE? WHAT'S HE ON ABOUT? WE NEED TO WIN, RIGHT? THREE POINTS OR THE SEASON ENDS AND BARRY CLEAVER SELLS OUR SOULS.
S'RIGHT.
WIN.
OH GOD. I FEEL A BIT SICK...

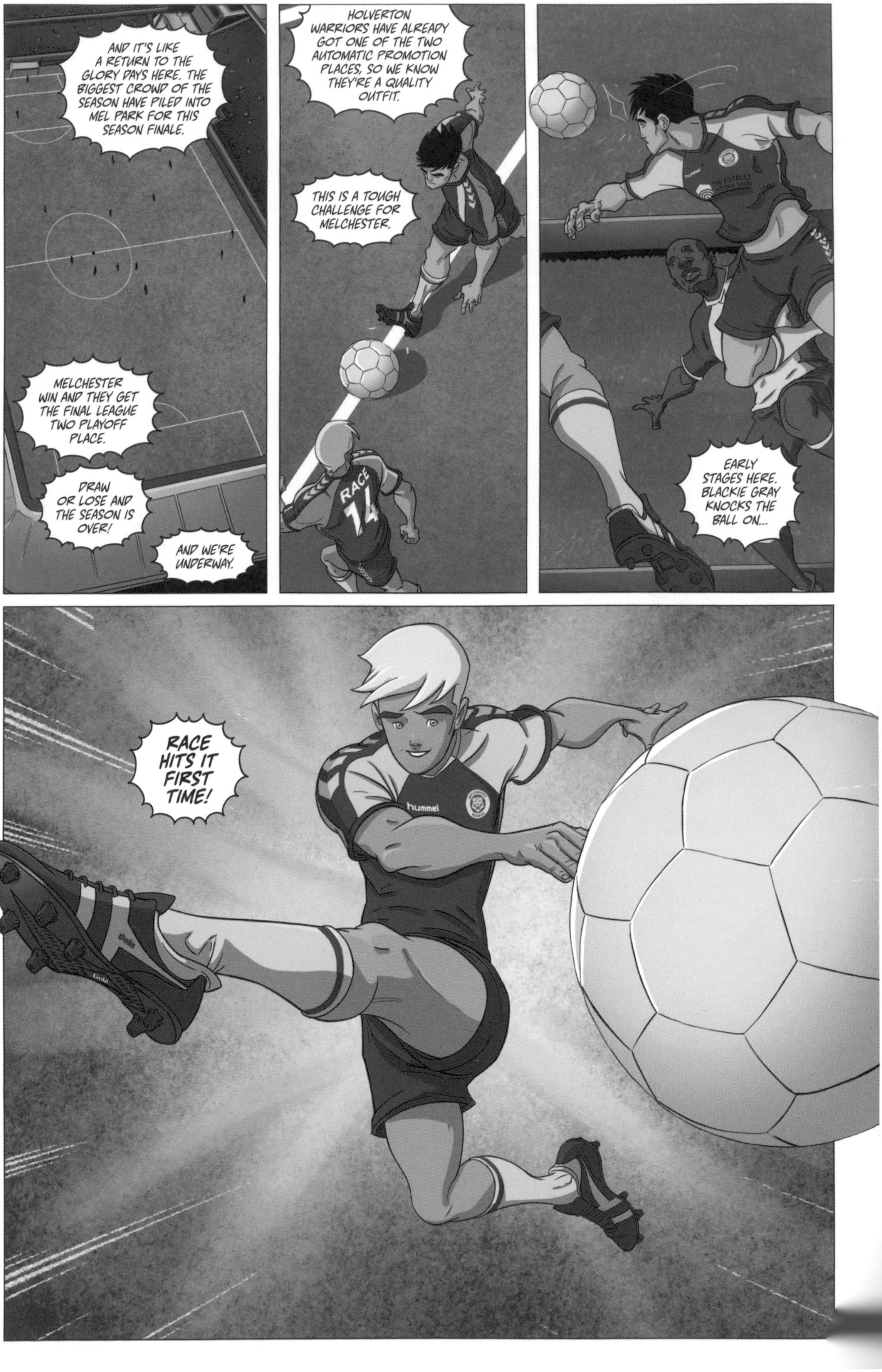
AND IT'S LIKE A RETURN TO THE GLORY DAYS HERE. THE BIGGEST CROWD OF THE SEASON HAVE PILED INTO MEL PARK FOR THIS SEASON FINALE.
MELCHESTER WIN AND THEY GET THE FINAL LEAGUE TWO PLAYOFF PLACE.
DRAW OR LOSE AND THE SEASON IS OVER!
AND WE'RE UNDERWAY.
HOLVERTON WARRIORS HAVE ALREADY GOT ONE OF THE TWO AUTOMATIC PROMOTION PLACES, SO WE KNOW THEY'RE A QUALITY OUTFIT.
THIS IS A TOUGH CHALLENGE FOR MELCHESTER.
RACE
14
EARLY STAGES HERE. BLACKIE GRAY KNOCKS THE BALL ON...
RACE HITS IT FIRST TIME!
hummel

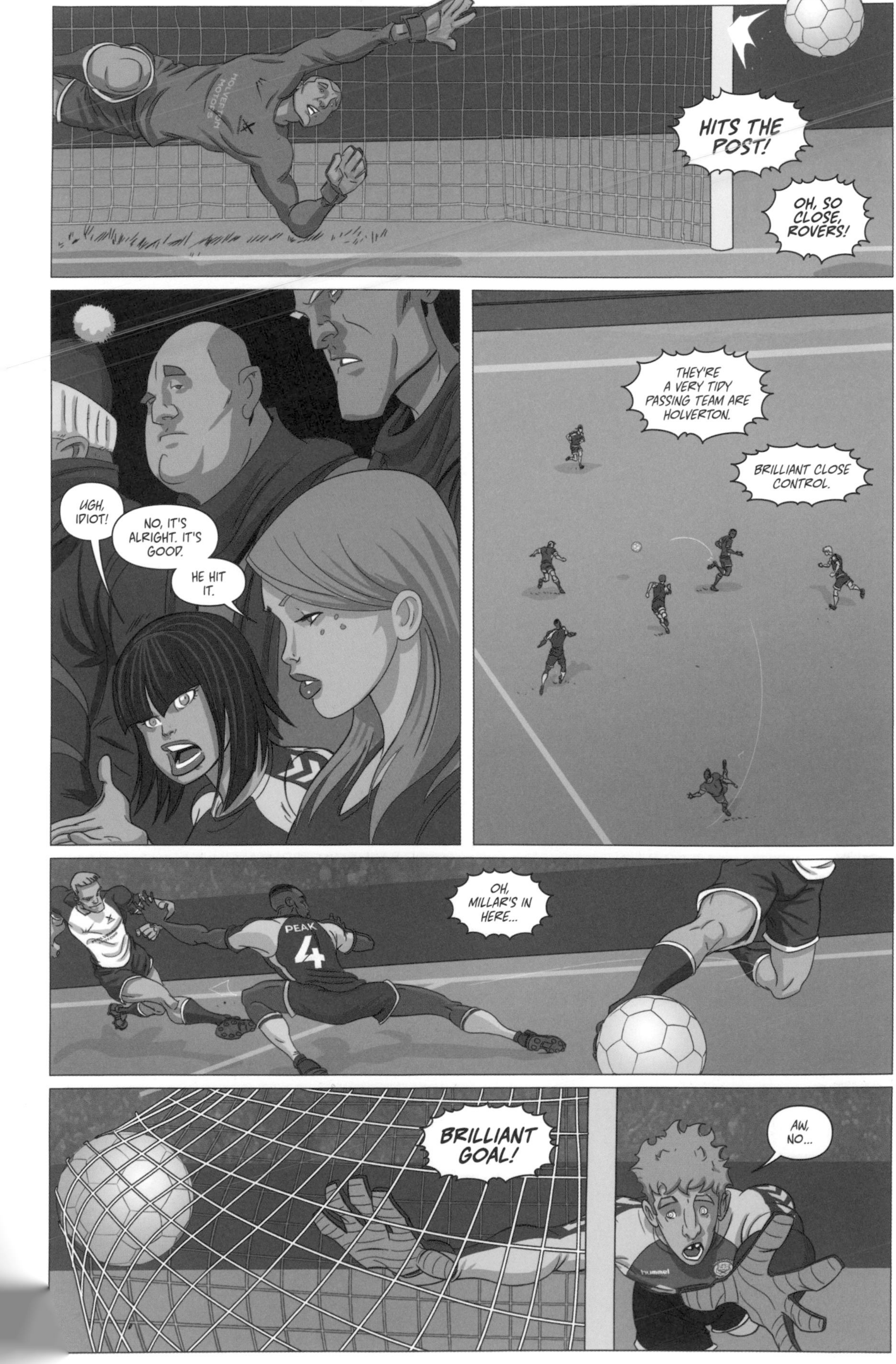
HOLVERTON MOTORS
HITS THE POST!
OH, SO CLOSE, ROVERS!
UGH, IDIOT!
NO, IT'S ALRIGHT. IT'S GOOD.
HE HIT IT.
THEY'RE A VERY TIDY PASSING TEAM ARE HOLVERTON.
BRILLIANT CLOSE CONTROL.
PEAK
4
OH, MILLAR'S IN HERE...
BRILLIANT GOAL!
AW, NO...
hummel

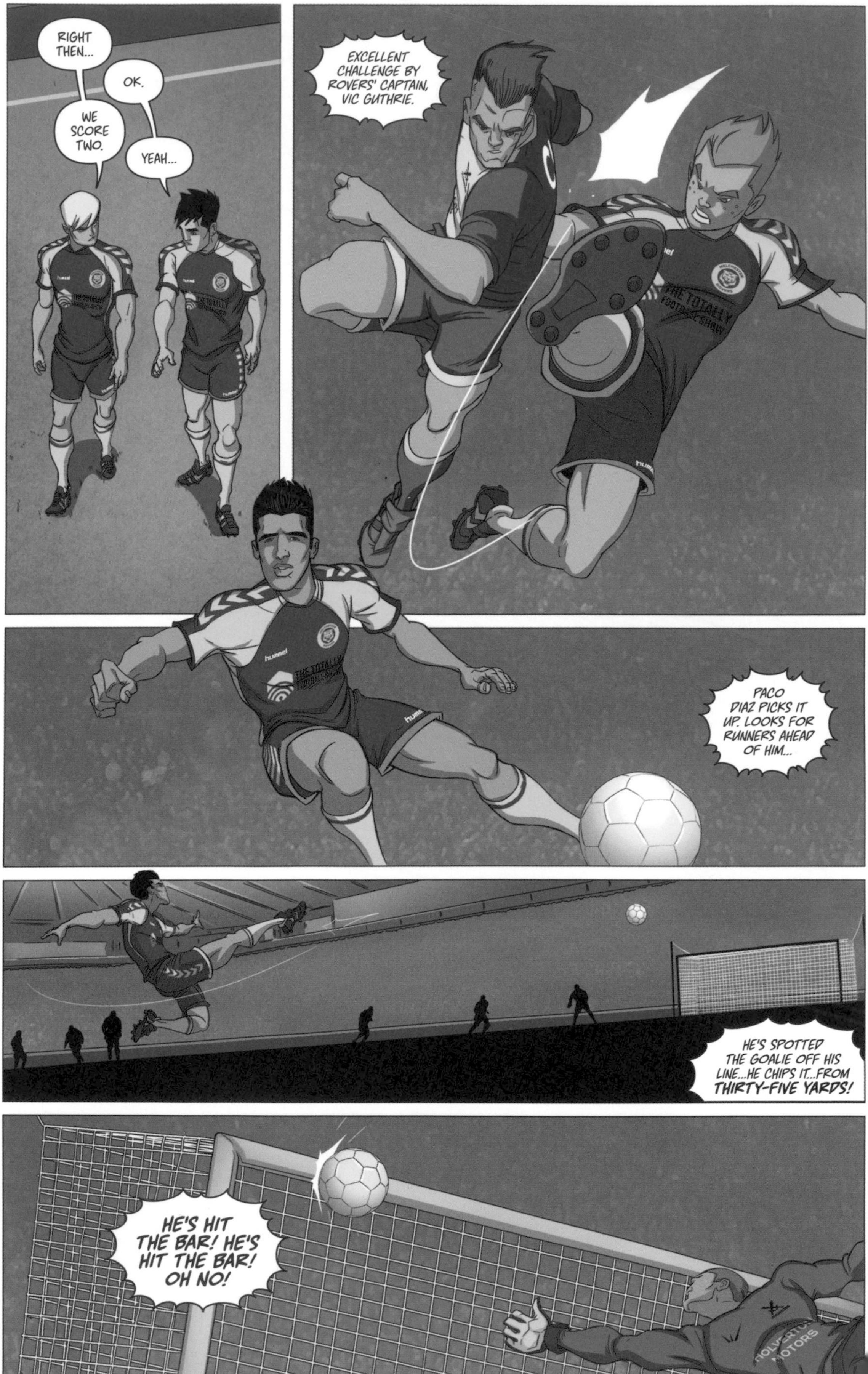
RIGHT THEN...
OK.
WE SCORE TWO.
YEAH...
EXCELLENT CHALLENGE BY ROVERS' CAPTAIN, VIC GUTHRIE.
PACO DIAZ PICKS IT UP. LOOKS FOR RUNNERS AHEAD OF HIM...
HE'S SPOTTED THE GOALIE OFF HIS LINE...HE CHIPS IT...FROM THIRTY-FIVE YARDS!
HE'S HIT THE BAR! HE'S HIT THE BAR! OH NO!

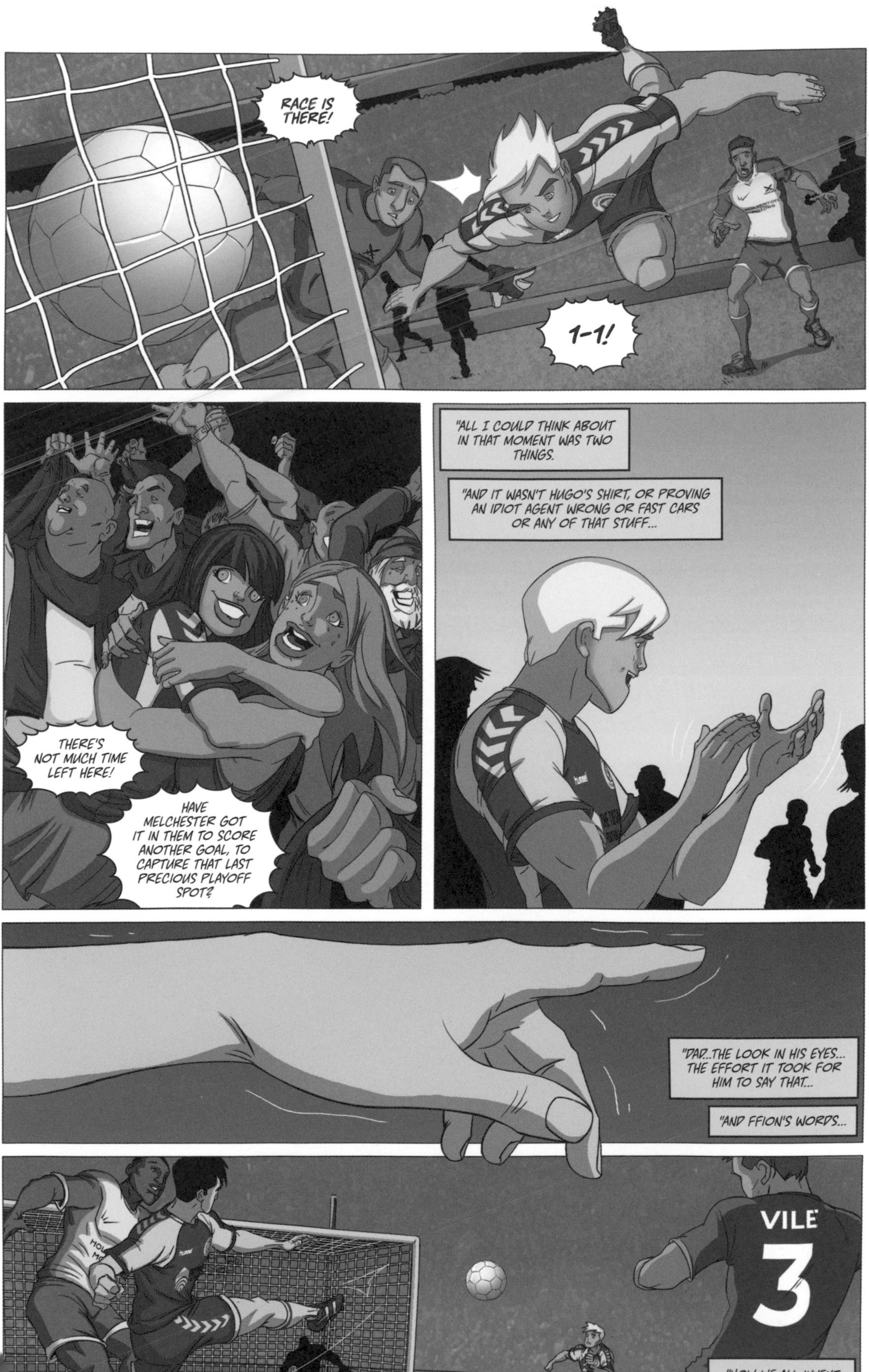
RACE IS THERE!
1-1!
THERE'S NOT MUCH TIME LEFT HERE!
HAVE MELCHESTER GOT IT IN THEM TO SCORE ANOTHER GOAL, TO CAPTURE THAT LAST PRECIOUS PLAYOFF SPOT?
"ALL I COULD THINK ABOUT IN THAT MOMENT WAS TWO THINGS.
"AND IT WASN'T HUGO'S SHIRT, OR PROVING AN IDIOT AGENT WRONG OR FAST CARS OR ANY OF THAT STUFF...
"DAD...THE LOOK IN HIS EYES... THE EFFORT IT TOOK FOR HIM TO SAY THAT...
"AND FFION'S WORDS...
VILE
3
"HOW WE ALL INVENT STORIES FOR OURSELVES..."

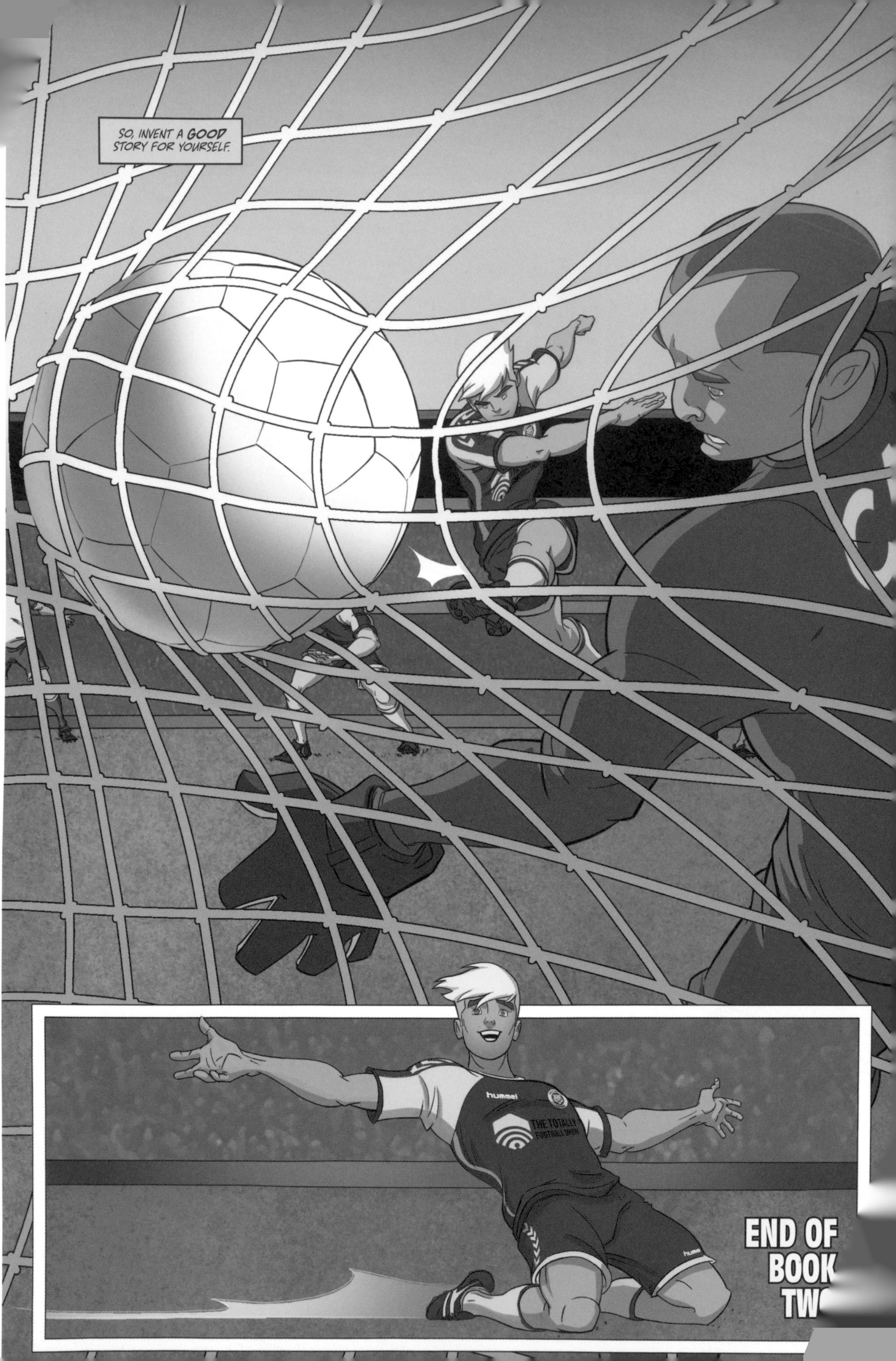
SO, INVENT A GOOD STORY FOR YOURSELF.
hummel
THE TOTALLY FOOTBALL SHOW
END OF BOOK TWO

MELCHESTER

ROVERS

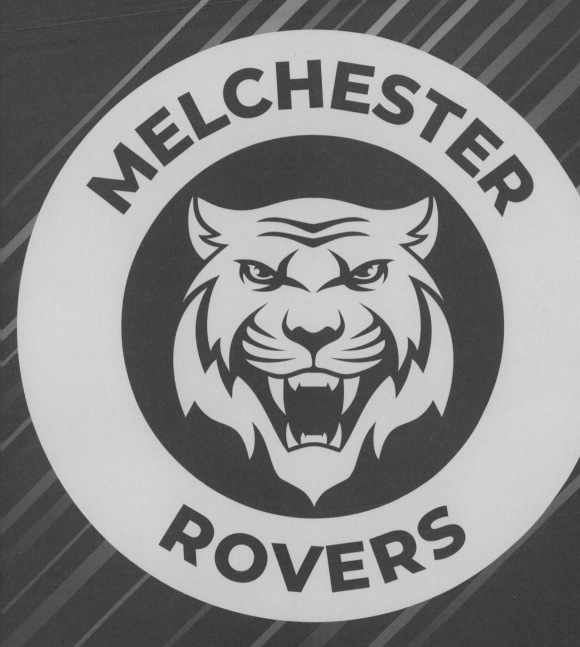

ROY OF THE ROVERS®
THE FIRST SEASON

Keep track of every new *Roy of the Rovers* book here!
Don't forget to tick the boxes as you read each one.

FICTION

BOOK 1	BOOK 2	BOOK 3
SCOUTED	**TEAMWORK**	**PLAYOFFS**
Author: Tom Palmer	Author: Tom Palmer	Author: Tom Palmer
Out: October 2018	Out: February 2019	Out: May 2019
ISBN: 978-1-78108-698-8	ISBN: 978-1-78108-707-7	ISBN: 978-1-78108-722-0
Roy Race is the most talented striker in Melchester – but is he good enough to catch the eye of the Melchester Rovers scouts?	Life gets tricky for Roy as he adjusts to life in the spotlight. Fortune and glory await, but can Roy juggle football, fame and family?	Crunch time for Rovers: the end of the season is here, the club is in deep trouble, and it's down to Roy to bring a bit of hope back to the Melchester faithful.
READ? ☐	**READ?** ☐	**READ?** ☐

GRAPHIC NOVELS

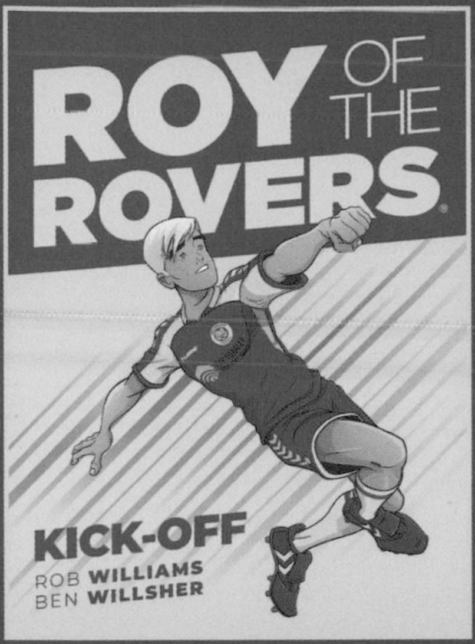
ROY OF THE ROVERS
KICK-OFF
ROB WILLIAMS
BEN WILLSHER

BOOK 1
KICK-OFF

Writer: Rob Williams
Artist: Ben Willsher
Out: November 2018
ISBN: 978-1-78108-652-0

Roy Race is 16, talented, and desperate to make it as a footballer. But is he good enough for Melchester Rovers? Now's the time to prove if he's got what it takes to become Roy of the Rovers.

READ? ☐

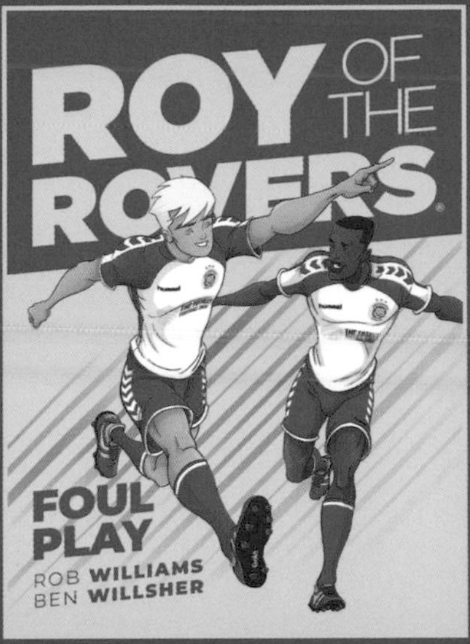
ROY OF THE ROVERS
FOUL PLAY
ROB WILLIAMS
BEN WILLSHER

BOOK 2
FOUL PLAY

Writer: Rob Williams
Artist: Ben Willsher
Out: March 2019
ISBN: 978-1-78108-669-8

Roy picks up an injury that puts him on the sidelines, and suddenly there's competition for his place as a brand new - and brilliant - striker is brought in by the management...

READ? ☐

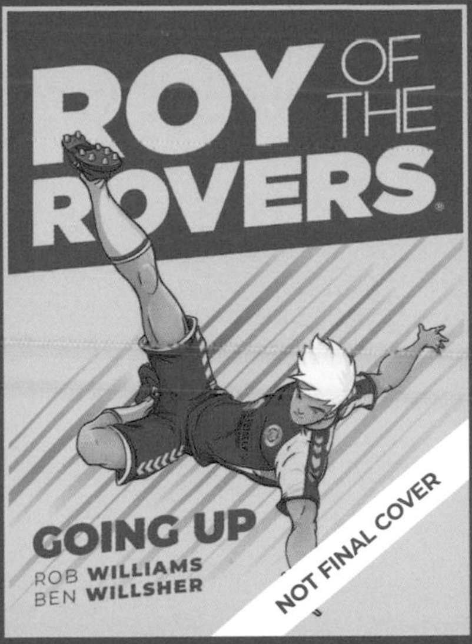
ROY OF THE ROVERS
GOING UP
ROB WILLIAMS
BEN WILLSHER
NOT FINAL COVER

BOOK 3
GOING UP

Writer: Rob Williams
Artist: Ben Willsher
Out: June 2019
ISBN: 978-1-78108-673-5

Roy and the team have battled through a tough season, but have they got enough left to get promoted? Or will they fall at the final hurdle and see the club sold by its greedy owner?

READ? ☐

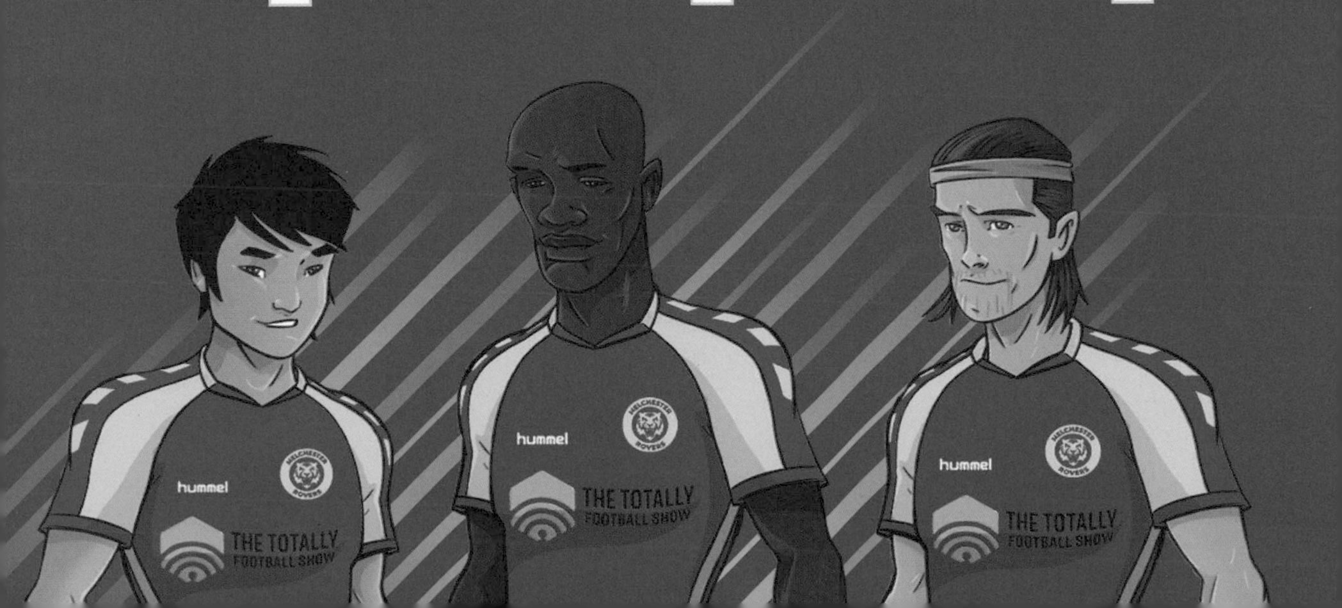
hummel
THE TOTALLY FOOTBALL SHOW

PLAYER INTERVIEW

Introduce Yourself

Hello. I'm Asif Mirza - right back for Melchester Rovers.

Do you have a nickname?

The lads just call me As.

Who was your favourite club growing up?

I'm a Melchester player so I really shouldn't say anything right? Okay, alright...I supported Deans Park. You're going to get me into trouble with the Gaffer!

Who is the best player that you have played with?

Wow, you're a trouble-maker! Only joking. I like playing with all the lads, but I feel that on the pitch I've really started to connect with Lofty. He makes us strong and stable.

Who is the best player that you have played against?

I give any forward or winger coming at me the same respect. If they get past me then the fault lies with me. So all of them and at the same time none of them. You look confused! Ha!

Do you have a pre-match routine?

I say a quiet prayer. Listen to some music. It all helps get me into the zone.

What's your advice to young players?

Never underestimate the opposition. And also, make sure you do your research on them before a game. Most strikers are creatures of habit - to know how they play allows you to stop them from playing.

What's your favourite social media network and why?

Snapchat. My brother puts pictures up of me doing my thing on the pitch. Luckily they disappear before it all becomes too embarrassing!

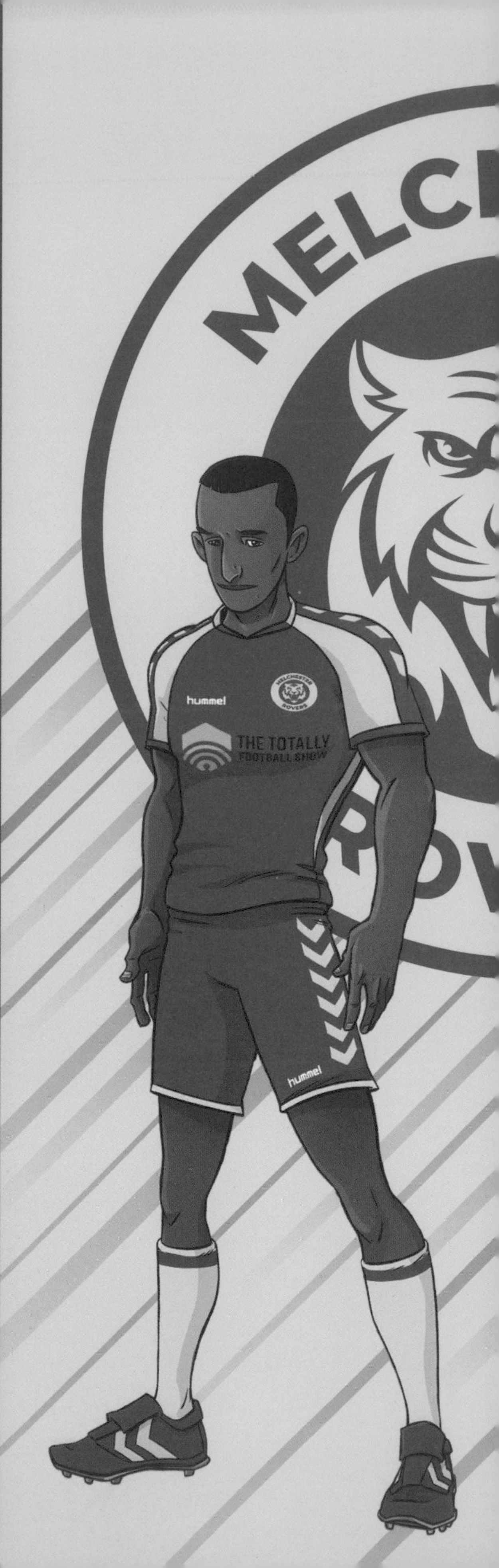
MELC
ROV
hummel
THE TOTALLY FOOTBALL SHOW
hummel

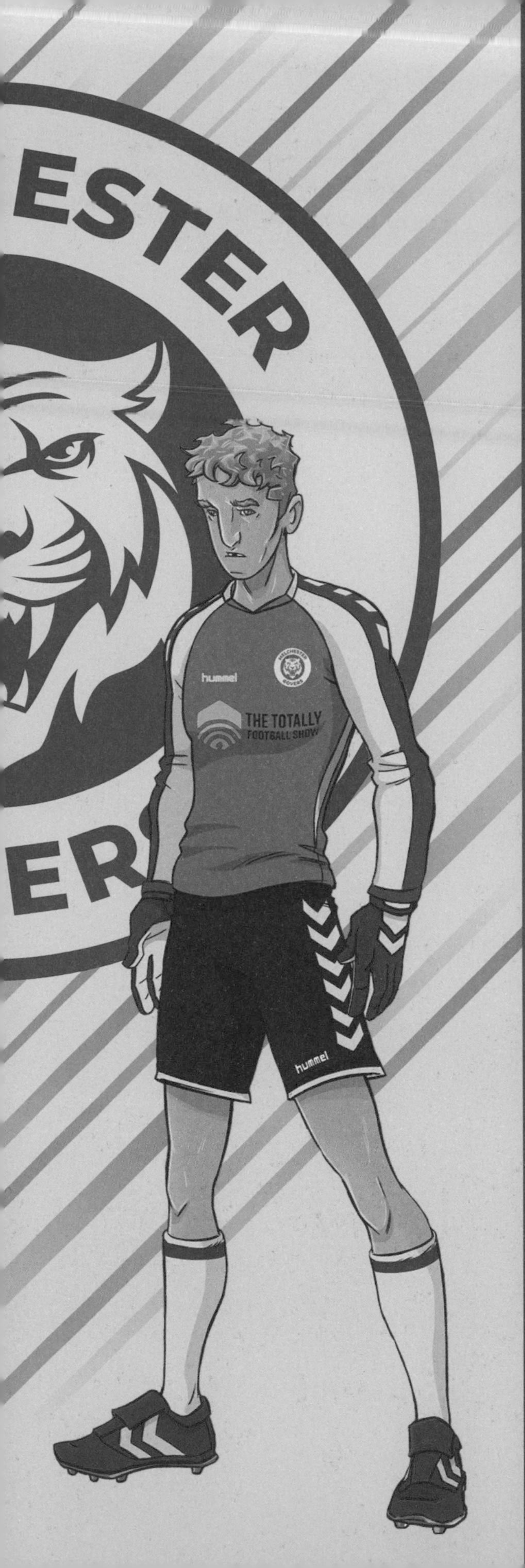
ESTER
ER
hummel
THE TOTALLY
FOOTBALL SHOW
hummel

PLAYER **INTERVIEW**

Introduce Yourself

Ah'm Gordon Stewart - otherwise known as the safest hands in Scotland!

Do you have a nickname?

Back home when I was playing for fun, it was Nessie, as in the big Scottish monster. The Melchester boys were calling me Big Man for a while, but then Lofty turned up!

Who was your favourite club growing up?

Princes Park- the pride of Scotland! Our bossman played there once and is an absolute legend at the club.

Who is the best player that you have played with?

At Melchester? I don't know. I can easily tell you who is the busiest player at the club though...me!

Who is the best player that you have played against?

Hands down, its that Hugo. I was dreading coming up against him in our cup tie with Tynecaster. I've seen him destroy some of the best keepers in the world. Thankfully, I came out of that game relatively unscathed. No, we didn't win, but we didn't get humiliated either.

Do you have a pre-match routine?

No liquids or food an hour before the game. I flick through an old Scotland international game on my phone just before we leave the dressing room - that usually gets me fired up!

What's your advice to young players?

To aspiring goalkeepers I'd say find your voice, use it to organise your defence. Defenders are like sheep that need herding and part of your job is to play farmer!

What's your favourite social media network and why?

I can't stop watching videos of goalkeeping blunders on YouTube.